Contents

Foreword by Ian Chapman   5
Foreword by George Alagiah   6
Foreword by Barbara Stocking   7
Introduction   8
Why I Got Involved with Fairtrade   10
My Personal Thanks   12
Conversion Chart   13

Recipes:
Light Bites   15
Comfort Food   33
A Taste of the East   53
Posh Nosh   75
Sweet Somethings   93
Chocoholics' Corner   129

Index   142

Special Thanks for
A Fair Feast

The publishers would like to thank the following for generously donating their services to this book:

Bright Arts Graphics (S) Pte Ltd

D&J Print Services

Fiona Andreanelli

HarperCollins Supply Chain

Hilo

Jonny Ring

KHL Printing Co Pte Ltd

Kim Yarwood

P&O Nedlloyd Limited

Paula Borton

Publiship

Royal Mail

Silver Chair

Spot on

Two Associates

A FAIR FEAST

70 CELEBRITY RECIPES FOR A FAIRER WORLD

COMPILED BY VICKY BHOGAL

SIMON & SCHUSTER
A VIACOM COMPANY

First published in Great Britain by Simon and Schuster UK Ltd, 2005
A Viacom Company
Copyright © 2005. All rights reserved.
Simon & Schuster UK Ltd, Africa House, 64–78 Kingsway, London WC2B 6AH

ISBN 0 7432-7598-5

Project management: Paula Borton
Design: Fiona Andreanelli, Jeremy Butcher
Cover design: Two Associates
Printed and bound in Singapore

1 3 5 7 9 10 8 6 4 2

Foreword from
Ian Chapman

When we were approached by our young cookery writer Vicky Bhogal with the idea for *A Fair Feast* it seemed to make so much sense. Many of our titles are cook books with wonderful ideas on food, and that's what, in many ways, the issue of global poverty is all about ...FOOD – ensuring people receive a fair price for the food they produce, so they can in turn provide food – and a future – for their families. So when the opportunity arose to create *A Fair Feast* in support of the Make Poverty History campaign it seemed such a positive stance against global poverty. And thank goodness others were as enthusiastic as we were. Busy chefs and celebrities took time to put together the most amazing array of recipes, our printers KHL Printing printed the book at no charge, our reproduction house Bright Arts donated their services, as did designers, editors and, of course, Vicky, who took time out of her busy schedule to compile the recipes. To everyone involved our most grateful thanks. We are delighted to donate proceeds to Oxfam and The Fairtrade Foundation. A worthy cause this may be but *A Fair Feast* is chiefly a celebration of food – so create these delicious recipes for your friends and family, eat, enjoy and rejoice in Making Poverty History.

Ian Chapman,
Managing Director and CEO,
Simon & Schuster UK Ltd

THE BRITISH PUBLIC ARE DRINKING OVER 3 MILLION CUPS OF FAIRTRADE HOT DRINKS A DAY AND MUNCHING THROUGH ALMOST HALF A MILLION FAIRTRADE BANANAS PER DAY.

**George Alagiah,
Patron, The Fairtrade
Foundation**

Guarantees
a **better deal**
for Third World
Producers

FAIRTRADE

Foreword from
The Fairtrade Foundation

These recipes are about culinary indulgence but without the guilt trip. In fact you can tell yourself that the more you eat the more good you'll be doing. Many recipes in this book contain produce that carries the FAIRTRADE Mark. There's no better guarantee that a fairer portion of the money you spend on the item will end up in the deserving hands of a farmer.

Just a few years ago a compilation as varied as this one would simply not have been possible. The range of Fairtrade products started with just three items in 1994. Now there are over 900 and by the time you try out your first recipe that number will certainly be out of date.

One other thing has changed. Gone are the days when Fairtrade was about conscience consuming – when you did it for the cause and not so much the taste. The quality of the ingredients has improved year by year. Today Fairtrade food is as scrumptious as it is ethical.

So at a time when we are bombarded with advice about what to eat, what not to eat and how to cut back on those things we can eat, it gives me huge pleasure to say – "Go ahead, tuck in and enjoy".

Foreword from
Oxfam

Barbara Stocking
Director, Oxfam

For more than 10 years Fairtrade has been an effective way to make a difference to the lives of people in developing countries through the consumer choices we make. Oxfam is delighted to be a recipient for the proceeds from this cookbook.

Fairtrade's success has been inspirational. It's a system based on quality: where we, the consumers, get the best quality products, guaranteeing producers a good quality of life.

However Fairtrade is only part of the solution to overcome poverty, the kind of poverty that takes a child's life every three seconds, leaves 1.3 billion people without access to clean water and 100 million children without an education.

Make Poverty History is a coalition of hundreds of organisations and millions of people across the UK tackling these issues head on, and calling for action from world leaders. Make Poverty History is building on the success of Fairtrade, and the Jubilee 2000 and Trade Justice Movements to call for action on trade justice, debt cancellation and more and better aid.

While developing countries are losing out on £375 billion every year in unfair trade, or paying more on debt repayments than on healthcare or education, poverty will remain.

With Oxfam I have travelled to many developing countries and heard how decisions taken in the hotels and conference centres of the rich world are devastating the lives of some of the world's poorest people. People like Inodil Fils, a small Haitian rice farmer who is struggling to feed his family thanks to the 'competition' of artificially cheap American rice dumped on his local markets. Or 12-year-old Adiatou Issaka from Niger who can't go to the school 500 metres from her house because it's full and her government is waiting for promised extra funding to build more schools and train more teachers.

Nelson Mandela compared Make Poverty History and the international coalition, the Global Call to Action Against Poverty, with the campaign to end slavery and the anti apartheid movement. Like those movements, we can succeed. We have a real opportunity to take action that will have a global impact, action that will Make Poverty History and make history.

FOUR-FIFTHS OF TOTAL GLOBAL CONSUMPTION EXPENDITURE IS ACCOUNTED FOR BY JUST ONE FIFTH OF THE WORLD'S POPULATION.

Introduction

Vicky Bhogal

Captured in its full colour glory on a simple home video is our family Christmas of 1984. Glinting foil snowflakes and wreaths of spiky tinsel hang from patterned walls; greetings cards emblazoned with smug, chubby robins and cartoon snowmen adorn every available scrap of surface; relatives bedecked in glitzy outfits, rivalled only by the baubled tree itself, scurry back and forth with trayfuls of steaming festive treats from the kitchen, dodging the littered offerings of torn crackers and children playing tag, weaving around the corduroy, polyester, silk and chiffon lower limbs of the towering grown ups, their little fingers perilously clutching cups of cherryade.

Amidst the mild chaos, is my 6-year-old self staring at the television screen, crisp paper hat jauntily perched atop my smooth bowl haircut, captivated by the music and images of the Band Aid video on the Top of the Pops Special. My parents, having noticed me bellowing out the infectious chorus whilst doing a rather frenzied little jig around the living room, explained the aim of the single to me in the most basic and simplest of terms - often the most effective way.

This memory came back to me in November 2004. I couldn't believe a whole 20 years had gone by in what seemed little more than a heartbeat. But more importantly, I couldn't believe that in those 20 years, there had been no improvement in Africa. Indeed, the situation in Africa, and on a wider level, global poverty itself, has only worsened. Fairer trade rules, more and better aid and the cancellation of Third World debts are needed to tackle world poverty. I was moved to find a way to contribute, but how?

As our finest singers geared up to put their tonsils to good use once again with the re-recording of the momentous single, I had a little idea.

The music industry has done so much to raise the awareness of world poverty and place it at the top of the political agenda. But what about the food industry? Chefs and food writers cook, eat, write or think about food almost all the time. We love to feed people, for that is what we are in the business of doing. What if we could combine our efforts and talents to help feed those who are truly in need and enable them to feed themselves and their families in the future?

The idea for *A Fair Feast* was born. A cookbook consisting of mouth-watering recipes donated from the biggest and best names in the food industry and a whole host of diverse celebrities, produced in conjunction with Oxfam and The Fairtrade Foundation, the proceeds of which go to projects to promote long-term food security, sustainable agriculture and the development of Fairtrade around the globe.

In January, having received the wholehearted support of Simon and Schuster, we all set to work to make this happen. The response was humbling and overwhelmingly generous as contributions came in thick and fast.

The book also rapidly became part of the newly launched Make Poverty History campaign. Make Poverty History brings together a wide cross section of organisations, trade unions and faith groups, united by a common belief that 2005 offers an unprecedented opportunity for global change on poverty, given that Britain has the presidency of the EU and is hosting the G8 this year, and is calling for more government action on trade, aid and debt.

By buying this unique collection of culinary gifts, you not only receive a wealth of glorious recipes, you also make your own gift of opportunity by feeding back to the hand that feeds us the much loved produce that has become part of our daily consumption. By showing us how superb Fairtrade ingredients can be used in a multitude of ways, becoming the food of choice for consumers the recipes in this book are not only recipes for delicious meals but also recipes for change. And as you will discover, change has never tasted so good!

Thank you so much for buying this book.

Why I Got Involved
With Fairtrade

My parents, like most other British Asian parents, instilled in me the value of working hard to achieve in life. As part of a generation who were skilled or educated back in their motherland of India, they often found themselves victims of prejudice and discrimination as immigrants.

Men who were doctors in India suddenly found themselves working in biscuit factories to earn a measly wage whilst women who had only known their family homes found themselves cleaning the toilet bowls of strangers.

The degrees of experience differed, but one thing was unquestionable. When these parents referred to working hard to achieve in life, they were not simply referring to educational success or financial prosperity alone. They were referring to a means by which to achieve respect, dignity, to be seen as equals and to achieve self-sufficiency.

I belong to a previously subjected people, the colonisation of whom was rooted in trade. A people who have fought and laboured for rights, success, progress and material comfort, and I therefore have empathy with those who are only asking for that very same right: to be able to work to achieve. To provide for their families, feed their children, invest in their countries and environment, work their way out of debt and poverty – to simply hold their heads high.

Zed Nelson

Howard Davies

They do not want charity, simply a fair reward for their hard work. It is very easy to become desensitised and dismiss the issue. To view it as something that happens 'over there' to 'those people' who live in 'those countries'.

Imagine if it were you. If you had spent hours toiling in blistering heat to be paid less than the cost of working in the first place.

There are many issues we cannot directly contribute towards in this world – this is not one of them. What is so empowering about Fairtrade is that each one of us has the potential to directly affect the lives and welfare of these people every day, and get something delicious out of it too.

It almost seems too easy to be true. But it is. Your consumer and commercial choices have an enormous impact and they will also benefit the global economy and contribute to international peace and security.

When I first heard of Fairtrade a few years ago, there was no turning back. And today there is more choice than ever with a range of products that are of extremely high quality.

I started with the tea bags. Coming from a typical British Asian family, I personally know how much British Asians love their sweet, hot, milky tea – or 'chaa' as we call it. As a teenager, I seemed to be forever making vatfuls for roomfuls of relatives and auntyjis. If every British Asian family switched to using Fairtrade tea bags, that would be a huge victory in itself!

My Personal Thanks

This book would simply not exist if it were not for the invaluable and generous support of and contribution from the following people, to whom I would like to offer my most sincere personal thanks:

All of the contributing chefs, food writers and celebrities who took the time to enthusiastically donate such wonderful recipes at hideously short notice, despite their relentless, frantic schedules! Also, their agents, PAs, publishers and press officers who are often overlooked but without whom this process would have been impossible. I thank them for being so incredibly helpful.

Janet Copleston and Kim Yarwood, who very kindly took the time to listen to my proposal, had utter faith in the project and made mountains move in order to produce this book. Paula Borton for project managing the entire publishing process and very kindly donating copy editing expertise. Sally Knowles and Katie Walsh for their tireless efforts.

Simon and Schuster UK, particularly Jeremy Butcher and Fiona Andreanelli who brought the book to life, Bob Ness, Kathy Gale, Sue Stephens and Emily Blickem.

My agents Euan Thorneycroft, Jacquie Drewe and Catherine Tapsell-Jenkin at Curtis Brown. This would have remained an idea fizzing away in my mind if it were not for your overwhelming support and absolute encouragement. Thank you for all your hard work.

Barbara Crowther at The Fairtrade Foundation. How you work so hard whilst always remaining so cool is beyond me! Thank you for your support and hard work, and that of Abi Murray and Eileen Maybin, and for helping to push this to an entirely different level from where we started.

Julie Wood at Oxfam. Thank you for committing yourself to this at a particularly frantic time and for all your help with every aspect of the book

Louise Doffman at Prospect Pictures, with whose help we avoided a logistical nightmare! Debora Robertson, Victoria Harper and Rosie Nixon at *Red* magazine — my three fairy godmothers who came to my rescue with a magic wand in the nick of time. Thank you for your help in making this happen. Lulu Grimes, thank you so much for your contacts and advice. Huge thanks also to Richard Curtis and Clare at Working Title for your wonderful support.

Thank you to my family for supporting me whilst I worked on this. An Internet connection and a telephone can go a long way!

Weight & Volume measures

Imperial (fluid ounces/pints)	Metric (millilitres/litres)	Imperial (ounces/pounds)	Metric (grams/kilograms)
1 fl oz	25 ml	1 oz	25 g
2 fl oz	50 ml	2 oz	50 g
3 fl oz	80 ml	3 oz	80 g
4 fl oz	115 ml	4 oz	115 g
5 fl oz	150 ml	5 oz	150 g
6 fl oz	175 ml	6 oz	175 g
7 fl oz	200 ml	7 oz	200 g
8 fl oz	225 ml	8 oz	225 g
9 fl oz	250 ml	9 oz	250 g
10 fl oz	300 ml	10 oz	275 g
11 fl oz	325 ml	11 oz	300 g
12 fl oz	350 ml	12 oz	350 g
13 fl oz	375 ml	13 oz	375 g
14 fl oz	400 ml	14 oz	400 g
15 fl oz	425 ml	15 oz	425 g
16 fl oz	450 ml	16 oz	450 g
17 fl oz	475 ml	1 lb 1 oz	475 g
18 fl oz	500 ml	1 lb 2 oz	500 g
19 fl oz	550 ml	1 lb 3 oz	525 g
20 fl oz/1 pint	575 ml	1 lb 4 oz	550 g
1 ¼ pint	700 ml	1 lb 5 oz	600 g
1 ½ pint	850 ml	1 lb 6 oz	625 g
1 ¾ pint	1 litre	1 lb 7 oz	650 g
2 pints	1.1 litres	1 lb 8 oz	675 g
2 ¼ pints	1.3 litres	2 lb	900 g
2 ½ pints	1.4 litres	3 lb	1.3 kg
2 ¾ pints	1.6 litres	3 lb 5 oz	1.5 kg
3 pints	1.7 litres		
3 ¼ pints	2 litres		

European wheat costs almost twice as much to produce as wheat from poor countries but – with the help of hand-outs from the European Union – it is dumped on poor countries at rock-bottom prices; pushing poor farmers out of business and into poverty.

Alanis Morissette - singer

light bites

Smoked Chicken, Mango & Herb Salad
with Toasted Brazils

Select mangoes that feel firm – too ripe and the flesh will mush as you finely slice. Bloody **delicious** this. And remember, and I'm not preaching, Fairtrade **helps** feed the hands that feed us with all these gorgeous things. We love our Asia, let's show it.

Serves 4

$^1/_2$ smoked, barbecue-roasted or regular cooked small chicken

juice of 1 Fairtrade lemon

1 $^1/_2$ tablespoons caster sugar

1 clove garlic, crushed

1 small hot chilli, very finely chopped

4 $^1/_2$ tablespoons rice vinegar

2 $^1/_2$ tablespoons Fairtrade clear honey

60 ml groundnut oil

1 teaspoon sesame oil

4 handfuls good feisty salad leaves (nothing fragile)

4 spring onions, shredded

2 handfuls coriander, mint and basil leaves

2 large firm Fairtrade mangoes, peeled and sliced into wafer thin slices

2 tablespoons lightly crushed roasted Fairtrade Brazil nuts (or peanuts)

Alastair Hendy

1. Flake the chicken meat into chunks and mix with the lemon juice, caster sugar, garlic, chilli and 3 tablespoons of the rice vinegar. Leave to marinate for a while whilst you prepare the dressing.
2. Put the honey and the remaining 1 $^1/_2$ tablespoons vinegar in a food processor and blend. Slowly add a thread of groundnut oil and sesame oil through the feed tube of the processor, continuing until fully homogenised with the honey mixture – like when making mayonnaise. The dressing should be of a runny honey consistency.
3. Gently fold the salad ingredients, spring onion and herbs with the chicken mixture.
4. Distribute the salad in piles onto plates or into bowls, top with sliced mango and dress lightly with the honey dressing and sprinkle with toasted Brazil nuts or peanuts.

A year ago, we didn't have any electricity in our houses. All the members of the Joint Body got together and discussed how we could pay to install it. Some money came from the Fairtrade premium and we each took out a loan. With electricity, my children can study at night. In the morning I can iron their clothes and we can use a hot plate for cooking. I am happy that Fairtrade helps me support my family.

Sivapackiam, Tea Picker, Sri Lanka

Victoria Woolhead

Giorgio Locatelli
Insalata di Agrumi – Fairtrade Citrus Salad

This lovely fruit salad can be eaten at breakfast, as a snack, and if you add a spoonful of lemon sorbet it becomes a **light and refreshing** dessert. Use Fairtrade fruit wherever you can.

Serves 4

2 unwaxed oranges
2 unwaxed tangerines
2 unwaxed mandarins
2 unwaxed clementines
100 ml (3.5 fl oz) water
50 g (2 oz) caster sugar, plus extra for dusting
1 clove

1. Using a vegetable peeler, pare the zest off the oranges, being careful not to remove the white pith, and place in a pan with the water, sugar and the clove. Bring to the boil, stirring until the sugar dissolves. Simmer for 4–5 minutes to make a light syrup, and then strain into a bowl.

2. Pare the zest off one tangerine, one mandarin and one clementine. If there is any white pith attached to the zest, scrape it off with a small, sharp knife. Finely shred the zest, then place in a small pan, cover with cold water and bring to the boil. Drain and repeat this process twice, to rid the zest of its bitterness.

3. Pour a quarter of the strained syrup into a small pan, add the blanched zest and simmer gently for 10 minutes. Strain the zest, then toss with some caster sugar until evenly coated. Transfer to a sheet of silicone or greaseproof paper and leave in a warm place to dry.

4. Meanwhile, peel and segment all the fruit and arrange on serving plates. Scatter the sugared citrus zest over the top, pour over the remaining syrup and chill before serving.

RICH COUNTRIES SPEND $1 BILLION A DAY ON AGRICULTURAL SUBSIDIES, PUTTING FARMERS IN POOR COUNTRIES OUT OF BUSINESS AND DRIVING DOWN THEIR INCOME.

David Selex
Fairtrade Avocado & Seaweed Salad with Ginger Soy Dressing

This is a cause I really believe in. So many farmers get a really raw deal in this world. It's a hard enough battle anyway without having to compete against farmers in the richest countries who receive untold subsidies; **that's very uncool** and I'm pleased to be able to do this to try at least to help redress the balance. This dressing is oil free and extremely versatile. It is very handy to have in the fridge as it has a long shelf life. It can be used for all sorts of green vegetable salads or noodle salads. It can **easily be converted** into a stir-fry seasoning with the addition of a little extra soy. In the restaurant we use this dressing with shellfish, fried tofu and vegetable dishes, hot and cold.

Serves 2

FOR THE SALAD
1 Fairtrade avocado
2 handfuls of green beans (trimmed and blanched)
2 tablespoons dried wakame seaweed (soaked in cold water and squeezed firmly)
1 red pepper (roasted and peeled)
1 tablespoon toasted sesame seeds (try to buy ready toasted for consistency)

FOR THE DRESSING
100 g water
100 g caster sugar
140 g rice wine vinegar
100 g dark soy sauce
15 g grated fresh ginger

1. To make the dressing, bring water and sugar to the boil in an appropriately sized pot. Add vinegar and soy sauce then remove from heat. Add the grated ginger when the liquid has cooled so that it retains its freshness.

2. Prepare all the salad ingredients, peel the avocado, blanch the green beans, peel the red pepper and soak and squeeze the wakame. Chop everything according to your preference – however, I suggest leaving the beans whole, cutting large strips of red pepper and big chunks of avocado.

3. Mix the prepared salad with a generous amount of dressing, scatter over the sesame seeds and serve.

NOTE: For a warmer main meal version, serve this salad on freshly steamed jasmine rice with either some fried tofu or sashimi (salmon or tuna).

Things have never been so good in this neighbourhood. Incomes are coming in from Fairtrade – there's a baseball pitch – a community canteen. Things are moving. I can save for that rainy day, so if I or one of the children get ill, I'll be able to solve the problem immediately. I feel very secure now – much more secure than before. I'll be grateful till my dying day.

Concepción, Banana Farmer, Dominican Republic

Free Trade, **or unfair trade?**

What we have now is a system of trade that is constructed, managed by and serves the vested interests of rich men in the global North, a system of rules and institutions that seeks to legitimise their actions and profits whilst ensuring they remain utterly unaccountable. Shocking, isn't it?

It is also a system that heavily contradicts itself. 'Free' trade in the North depends for its very survival upon:

- **government subsidies** the rich world spends $1 billion a day on subsidising (with taxpayers' money) its own farming the produce of which it dumps on developing countries, forcing down the price of their local produce

- **the closure of their markets** to exports from the South whilst simultaneously forcing poor countries to open their markets to Northern exports, dumping their subsidised produce upon them. The World Trade Organisation's rules are biased towards rich transnational corporations whilst slapping developing countries with huge costs.

Not exactly what I would call free competition. It is time to open our eyes.

Georgia Glynn Smith

Sir Terence & Vicki Conran
Kedgeree

We like this as a scratch dish, that is to say not made from leftover fish or rice. Traditionally served for breakfast, it makes a **very good** light lunch or supper.

Serves 4

500 g smoked haddock
splash of sunflower oil
1 large onion, finely chopped
200 g basmati rice
1 teaspoon curry powder or paste
2 tablespoons double cream
40 g butter
small handful of finely chopped parsley
4 eggs, hard-boiled, shelled and kept in a basin
  of very hot water
mango chutney, to serve

1. Cook the smoked haddock in barely simmering water for about 5 minutes. Lift the fish from the liquid (reserve this), remove the bones and skin and then flake the fish.
2. Heat the oil in a large sauté pan, add the onion and fry gently until it is transparent and just becoming golden.
3. Stir in the rice and about 500 ml of the water in which the fish was cooked, and the curry powder or paste. Bring the whole lot to the boil. Then cover the pan and simmer for 10–12 minutes, or as directed on the packet, until the rice is just tender.
4. Stir in the double cream and the butter into the cooked rice, and then gently fold in the flaked fish and the chopped parsley. Check the seasoning.
5. Quarter the eggs.
6. Serve the kedgeree on very hot plates, topped with the egg quarters. Mango chutney is the perfect accompaniment.

Debbie Rowe

Iain Philpott

Fiona Beckett
Fairtrade White Sangria

*If students can buy Fairtrade products out of their limited budget as I know they do, through my student website www.beyondbakedbeans.com, there's **no excuse** for the rest of us not to. This is a bit like a floating fruit salad but brilliantly refreshing. There are a good few Fairtrade wines around now – mostly from South Africa. Use a simple dry white to make this deliciously refreshing version of Sangria.*

Makes a large jugful

1 bottle Fairtrade dry white wine, chilled
1 x 5 cl miniature Cointreau or other orange-flavoured liqueur
2 tablespoons caster sugar
$\frac{1}{2}$ Fairtrade orange and $\frac{1}{2}$ Fairtrade lemon, finely sliced
$\frac{1}{4}$ ripe honeydew melon, peeled and cut into cubes
chilled soda water to taste

1. Pour the wine into a large jug with the Cointreau and sugar and stir till the sugar has dissolved.
2. Add the orange and lemon slices and leave to infuse for an hour or so.
3. Add the melon and 10–12 ice cubes and then top up with soda to taste.

Dr Gillian McKeith
Mango Mania

*This is my **Number One** top favourite smoothie. It's very filling, tastes heavenly and it's a great way to get your bowels going.*

Serves 1–2

1 large Fairtrade mango, peeled, stoned and roughly chopped
2 Fairtrade bananas, peeled and roughly chopped
1 serving of Dr Gillian McKeith's Living Food Energy Powder
1 handful each of blueberries and raspberries, to serve

1. Blend the mango, bananas and Living Food Energy Powder until smooth and creamy.
2. Put the blueberries and raspberries in a tall glass, reserving a few raspberries.
3. Pour the smoothie over the berries and serve garnished with the reserved raspberries.

Ellen Von Unwerth

Katharine Hamnett
Anti-Anthrax Salad Dressing, Food as Medicine

After September 11, when we all thought we were going to be anthraxed, I learnt that not everybody exposed to anthrax gets it, your only defence is to have a powerful immune system. This recipe boosts your immune system. Garlic is a **fantastic tonic** and natural antibiotic. This dressing also keeps away colds and flu. Cheap, delicious, amazingly good for you and quite posh.

Serves 4

15 cloves of garlic, finely chopped to dust (not crushed)
2 tablespoons of balsamic vinegar
$\frac{1}{2}$ teaspoon salt
1 teaspoon of toasted sesame oil and or walnut oil
8 tablespoons of olive oil
4 organic Little Gem lettuces (washed)

1. Soak the garlic in the vinegar and salt for 10 minutes (soaking in vinegar takes the bite out of the garlic).
2. Mix in the oil and beat to an emulsion. Pour the mixture over the drained lettuce leaves, toss and serve.

NOTES
Eating this quantity of garlic at once any other way would be impossible, it would make you faint, kill you, blow your head off or send you screaming to the bathroom in agony as garlic burns.

- Add a handful of finely chopped parsley if you are afraid of reeking of garlic (chlorophyll acts as a breath freshener).
- Add hard boiled eggs for a more substantial salad.
- Add roasted peppers, roasted butternut, fried pine nuts, avocado, or stir-fried cavalla nero or spring greens (hot) for a complete meal.

This is a very, very, very easy thing to make, the easiest thing in the whole world. **Easier than toast** and that's really easy. You can serve it with millions of things. Here are some suggestions: baked potato; salad; baked potato AND salad; mango, ginger and chilli coulis (mash a mango, add finely chopped ginger and chilli); bed of wilted spinach – don't go for this myself but some do; broccoli and sweet potato – loads of things!

Serves 2

2 tuna steaks
2 limes
sunflower oil for frying

Mark Mccall

Marian Keyes
Easier-Than-Toast Tuna

1. Put tuna in a bowl, squeeze some lime juice over them, leave to marinate in the fridge for as long as you can.
2. Put a heavy frying pan or wok on a high heat, add sunflower oil, when oil is smoking add tuna steaks, reserving lime juice. Sear on both sides. Cook for a few minutes depending on how rare or well done you like it.
3. Just before you take the tuna out, add the rest of the lime juice. It will all fizz up and bubble, like something a mad scientist has in a test tube, and will reduce very quickly to almost nothing. Make sure the tuna is covered in the reduced sauce. Serve!

Dido
Banana, Celery & Curry Powder Salad (this is not a joke)

My Mum used to give us this salad and it's **surprisingly okay.**

Serves as many as you like

celery
olive oil
Fairtrade bananas
curry powder
lemon juice

1. Chop up some celery, put it into a bowl and add a little bit of olive oil.
2. Chop an equal amount of Fairtrade bananas into small slices. Add to bowl.
3. Add a spoonful of curry powder. You might want to add more or less, depending on taste.
4. You can also squeeze a little bit of lemon on to stop the bananas from going brown.
5. Eat.

Ellen Von Unwerth

Minnie Driver
Glamorous Fruit

This is one of my favourite simple brunch dishes from my aunt's cookbook, *Serena, Food & Stories* by Serena Bass. The mangoes in the recipe must be Fairtrade. **Enjoy!**

Serves 6

2 Fairtrade mangoes, chilled
2 Asian pears, chilled
1 bunch perky mint, 10 of the leaves cut into fine
    shreds just before you need them, and the rest
    reserved for decoration

1. Peel the mangoes and cut into diagonal $^3/_4$ inch chunks.
2. If the Asian pears have a thin skin, you can leave it on; otherwise, peel the pears before cutting. Cut the pears the same way and toss both fruits with the shredded mint.
3. Use the rest of the bunch of mint for decoration. Happily, Asian pears don't turn brown like other pears when they are left out for a while.

Joanne Harris

Mango & Avocado Salad with Sticky Balsamic

*This is my daughter's favourite salad, and it works wonderfully well, either as a quick meal in itself with nachos or chilli-garlic bread, or as an elegant and colourful starter to a **celebratory** dinner. It's so simple a child can make it, but very effective, and the combination of luscious avocado and sweet, ripe mangoes needs very little to enhance it but a dash of good balsamic vinegar and a healthy appetite…*

Serves 4

generous handful of pine nuts
olive oil for toasting
3 small organic avocados (not too ripe)
3 small or medium Fairtrade organic mangoes
1 ripe organic lime
good quality balsamic vinegar

1. Mix the pine nuts with a little olive oil and place in the oven on a baking tray to toast for five minutes, or until nicely golden.
2. Meanwhile, peel the avocados and mangoes and slice them lengthways into generous pieces. Mix and arrange them on a plate – but avoid damaging the delicate fruit.
3. Add a generous squeeze of lime juice, a drizzle of the stickiest balsamic vinegar you can get your hands on, and scatter the toasted pine nuts over the top.

NOTE: Make sure you choose avocados that are still firm, and mangoes that are ripe, but not overly so.

Sheila Hancock
Donation Delight

I am such a rotten cook that I won't inflict anything on people and can best help by sending a **donation**!! I'm sure everyone will enjoy cooking all these other lovely recipes instead.

Fairtrade has been the saviour of the farmers in Dominica – of agriculture and the whole economy. With Fairtrade, small farmers have been transformed from marginalized farmers into businessmen.

Amos Wiltshire, Banana Grower, Dominica

25 million
growers face
ruin because
they don't get a
decent price for
their coffee –
yet some of the
world's biggest
coffee
companies
continue to
make big profits.

Colin Firth - actor

comfort food

Yasmin Alibhai-Brown
Kheema Potato Pie

The British abroad during the days of the **Empire** tried to eat as if they had never left the motherland, using imported products that often arrived stale and unpleasant. Maybe this is why, in the end, they did take up some of the foods of the places they ruled and incorporated them into their repertoires. The colonised, in turn, appropriated 'English food' and modified it to suit their palates. This is one such example – Indian shepherd's pie. Both **my children loved it** from the moment they learnt to eat real food. As I did as a child.

Serves 4

FOR THE FILLING

1 lb very lean mince
salt
³/₄ teaspoon crushed ginger
³/₄ teaspoon crushed garlic
³/₄ teaspoon garam masala
6 spring onions, finely chopped
1 bunch fresh coriander, chopped
2 green chillies, finely chopped
juice of 1 small lime
³/₄ teaspoon mint sauce
5 tomatoes, chopped

FOR THE MASH

8 medium-sized potatoes
50 g butter
¼ teaspoon crushed garlic
5 tablespoons double cream
2 tablespoons milk
³/₄ teaspoon paprika powder
salt to taste

1. For the mash, peel and halve the potatoes and put them on to boil in salty water.
2. Using a non-stick frying pan, dry fry the mince with salt, ginger and garlic.
3. Add garam masala and cook for two more minutes until dry and aromatic. Allow to cool.
4. Add the finely chopped spring onions, coriander, green chillies and lime juice, as well as the mint sauce. Transfer into a pie dish and layer the tomatoes over the top.
5. Melt 40 g of the butter and add the garlic, frying it over a gentle heat for a minute.
6. Mash the potatoes with this butter and garlic mixture, and add all the other ingredients. Spread the mash over the meat and tomato mixture. Melt the remaining 10 g of butter and brush over the top.
7. Bake for 25 minutes in the oven at a medium temperature (Gas Mark 4/180°C/350°F) until brown on top. Serve with tomato ketchup for the children.

Barney Desmazery
Slow-cooked Pork with Celeriac & Orange

This is one of those big-flavoured, slow-cook dishes where the meat just falls apart. The orange zest adds sweetness to the finished dish, counterbalancing the earthy flavours of the celeriac and leek. Slow cooking is like the **magic formula** for turning tough stewing meat into the most meltingly tender pieces.

Serves 6

3 leeks
2 carrots
3 tablespoons olive oil
900 g (2 lbs) boneless pork, cut into large
    stewing pieces (shoulder is an ideal
    cut to use)
2 small or 1 large celeriac (about 1 kg/2 lb 4 oz),
    peeled and diced into large chunks
2 garlic cloves, chopped
200 ml (7 fl oz) dry white wine
200 ml (7 fl oz) chicken stock
juice and peel of 1 Fairtrade orange (remove the
    orange peel with a potato peeler)
2 tablespoons soy sauce, Kikkoman is good
large sprig of rosemary
salt and freshly ground black pepper
crusty bread, to serve

1. Preheat oven to Gas Mark 1/140°C/fan oven 120°C. Trim and wash the leeks and cut each into about five pieces. Peel and chop the carrots into pieces the same size as the leeks. Heat a large-lidded flameproof casserole dish on top of the stove until it is very hot. Add 2 tablespoons of the olive oil and then carefully tip the pork into the casserole dish and leave it for a couple of minutes to brown. Stir once, then leave for another couple of minutes. Using a slotted spoon, remove the meat to a plate. Pour the rest of the oil into the pan, tip in all the vegetables, then fry for 3–4 minutes, stirring, until they start to brown. Add the garlic and fry for a minute more.

2. Stir the pork and any juices into the vegetables, and then pour in the wine, stock, orange juice and soy sauce. Throw in the rosemary and orange zest, season with salt and pepper, give it a stir, then bring everything to the boil.

3. Cover the pot, transfer it to the oven and cook for 2 hours, stirring after an hour. Cook until the pork is very tender and the leeks fall apart when prodded with a spoon. (The pork dish can now be left to cool and then frozen for up to 1 month.) Leave the dish to stand for at least 10 minutes, then spoon straight from the casserole into bowls. Serve with hunks of crusty bread to soak up the juices.

Mary Cadogan
Lamb with Lemon & Dill

Shut out the cold, light the fire and cosy up with this one-pot feast for two. It can be made up to three days ahead and reheats **wonderfully** well, plus you can double or even treble the quantities for larger numbers. Oh, and it also freezes well.

Serves 2

350 g (12 oz) ready diced lamb
2 teaspoons plain flour
1 tablespoon sunflower oil
1 onion, chopped
300 ml (¹/₂ pint) hot chicken or vegetable stock
3 tablespoons chopped fresh dill
1 bay leaf
300 g (10 oz) salad potatoes, thickly sliced
zest and juice of half a Fairtrade lemon
2 tablespoons crème fraîche
salt and freshly ground black pepper

1. Toss the lamb in the flour with a little salt and plenty of freshly ground black pepper. Heat the oil in a heavy-based pan, add the onion and fry for 5 minutes until softened. Add the lamb and stir well until it is tinged brown.
2. Stir in the stock, 2 tablespoons of the dill and the bay leaf. Bring to the boil, then simmer for 30 minutes.
3. Add the potatoes and lemon juice and cook for a further 30 minutes until the potatoes are tender. Serve in soup plates or individual dishes with a spoonful of crème fraîche and a scattering of lemon zest and dill on each serving. Some crusty bread on the side will be useful for mopping up all the juices.

Trade & Poverty

We have all heard the government rhetoric making commitments towards reducing world poverty. Yet, whilst one hand pledges to deliver aid, the other hand robs them of twice as much in unfair tariffs and debt repayments. This strategy blocks the escape route from poverty that trade offers. International trade rules are part of the problem of global poverty. However, they could be part of the solution.

Nelson Mandela in London at the launch of the Make Poverty History campaign stated 'like slavery and apartheid, poverty is not natural'; well, neither is the international trade system in its current form. It too 'is man-made' and can instead be used as a force for eradicating poverty and creating a system based on shared values of social justice, not charity.

The Trade Justice Movement

Both the Fairtrade Foundation and Oxfam are members of the Trade Justice Movement, a network of over 60 organisations and part of Make Poverty History. Together we are calling on the UK Government to:

* fight to ensure that governments, particularly in poor countries, can choose the best solutions to end poverty and protect the environment
* end export subsidies that damage the livelihoods of poor communities around the world
* make laws that stop big business profiting at the expense of poor people and the environment.

For more information on the Trade Justice campaign, visit www.tjm.org.uk

KarlGrant.Com

Carol Vorderman

Sweetcorn & Butter Bean Chowder with Green Chilli Cornbread

This is a favourite recipe of mine, **especially** on a cold winter's day.

Serves 4

FOR THE CHOWDER
2 tablespoons (30 ml) extra virgin olive oil
1 onion, chopped
1 clove garlic, crushed
2 potatoes, peeled and diced
600 ml (1 pint) vegetable stock
600 ml (1 pint) skimmed milk
420 g (14 oz) tinned sweetcorn, drained
420 g (14 oz) tinned butter beans, drained
freshly ground black pepper

FOR THE CORNBREAD
175 g (6 oz) cornmeal
1 tablespoon (15 ml) baking powder
$\frac{1}{2}$ teaspoon (2.5 ml) low-sodium salt
2 eggs
2 tablespoons (30 ml) rapeseed or sunflower oil
250 ml (9 fl oz) soya milk or yogurt
1–2 canned or pickled chillies, chopped
   (according to your taste)

1. Preheat the oven to Gas Mark 4/180°C/350°C.

2. First make the cornbread. Mix together the cornmeal, baking powder and salt in a large bowl. In a separate bowl combine the eggs, oil and soya milk or yogurt.

3. Add the wet mixture to the cornmeal mixture and mix together. Add the chopped chillies and pour into a lightly oiled 20 cm x 20 cm baking dish.

4. Bake for 25 minutes or until the cornbread is coming away from the sides of the dish and it is risen and golden.

5. While the cornbread is baking, make the chowder. Heat the olive oil in a large pan. Add the onion and garlic and cook over a moderate heat for 5 minutes.

6. Add the potatoes and the stock. Bring to the boil, reduce the heat then simmer for 10 minutes. Add the remaining ingredients and simmer for a further 10 minutes, stirring occasionally. Season with freshly ground pepper to taste. Serve piping hot with the cornbread.

FOR EVERY DOLLAR GIVEN TO POOR COUNTRIES IN AID, THEY LOSE TWO DOLLARS TO RICH COUNTRIES BECAUSE OF UNFAIR TRADE BARRIERS AGAINST THEIR EXPORTS.

Joan Collins
Joan's Fairtrade Supper

Fadie Berisha

This is an **extremely simple** but very delicious dish which I make especially for when the family are visiting. Since I am not a professional cook I just use imagination as far as exact amounts are concerned.

Serves 2–4

1 medium chicken
sausagemeat
virgin olive oil
onions
small potatoes
salt
Fairtrade mangoes, to serve
broccoli, to serve

1. Stuff the chicken with sausagemeat.
2. Put it in a large roasting pan and liberally cover with virgin olive oil – a lot! And a pinch of salt.
3. In the same pan, put several onions, sliced, and several small potatoes.
4. Place the pan in the oven on a medium heat and baste every 15 minutes. If the olive oil dries up, put in more.
5. Serve with sliced Fairtrade mangoes and broccoli.

Hugh Fearnley-Whittingstall
Citrus-braised Lamb Shanks

The standard version of this dish is rich and red-winey – pleasant, but I prefer something **fresher** and **zestier**.

Serves 4

2 to 3 tablespoons olive oil
1 carrot, diced
1 onion, diced
2 celery sticks, diced
few sprigs of thyme
2 bay leaves
2 garlic cloves, chopped
1 tablespoon tomato purée
¹/₂ botttle white wine (Fairtrade if you have it)
250 ml lamb stock
juice and zest of a Fairtrade lemon
juice and zest of a Fairtrade orange
4 lamb shanks
salt and freshly ground black pepper
bunch of parsley, chopped, to garnish

1. Heat some of the oil in a large casserole dish, add the vegetables and sweat, without browning, until tender.
2. Add the herbs, garlic, purée, wine and stock, along with most of the citrus juice and zest (retain a few pinches of zest and a tablespoon of each juice).
3. Bring to the boil, then reduce the heat to a gentle simmer.
4. Heat a little more oil in another pan and brown the shanks on all sides, seasoning as you go. Place them in the dish and put the lid on.
5. Transfer to a low oven (Gas Mark 1 or 2/ 120°C/250°F/) and cook for 2 ¹/₂ hours, until the meat is tender and falling off the bone.
6. Remove the shanks from the pan and keep warm.
7. To make a sauce, skim off some of the fat from the liquid left in the casserole. Taste the liquid and adjust the seasoning. If it's too thin, boil to reduce it, then stir in the reserved lemon and orange juice.
8. Serve the lamb on warmed plates with the sauce spooned over, and sprinkle with parsley and citrus zest. Accompany with mashed potatoes, wet polenta or some creamy beans such as butter beans or cannellini.

Gillian Carter
Pea & Leek Risotto

Serves 2

1 leek
200 g risotto rice (Arborio, Carnaroli or Vialone nano)
1 litre vegetable or chicken stock (I use Marigold bouillon powder)
150 g frozen peas, petis pois give a lovely sweet and tender result
1 tablespoon olive oil
50 g butter
small wine glass of vermouth (bianco) or glass of white wine
chunk of parmesan to grate in at the end – as much as you like
parsley, to serve

Risotto is my absolute favourite comfort food, and depending on what you add to it, it works just as well in summer or winter. Risotto-making is quite labour intensive, but it's also **relaxing**, with lots of therapeutic gentle stirring best done to music of your choice.

1. Get your ingredients ready. First, remove the leek's tough outer green leaves and chop the rest into 1 cm thick slices. Rinse the pieces under running water in a colander to remove any dirt.

2. Measure out your rice, and add a litre or so of boiling water to your stock powder (or use a litre of your own stock) and pour into a medium-sized saucepan. Put the pan on the lowest heat so your stock will gently simmer as you make the risotto.

3. Get the peas out of the freezer and measure into a cup or bowl.

4. Add the oil and half the butter to a medium-sized frying or sauté pan, and heat it on the hob. After a minute add the leeks and sweat them on a medium heat until they're translucent – don't let them get brown. Now add all the rice, stirring with a wooden spoon so every grain becomes shiny with oil.

5. Turn up the heat a fraction and throw in your vermouth or wine, letting it bubble for a minute, stirring all the time, making sure you sweep up grains of rice on the sides of the pan. When the liquid has evaporated, turn the temperature down to a simmer again, and add a good ladleful of the stock, continuing to stir. Keep adding stock every few minutes or so once the previous ladleful has evaporated.

6. After 10 minutes add your frozen peas to the stock, turning up the heat high so as not to lower the temperature of the stock for too long. As soon as it gets back up to boiling point turn it down.

7. Keep adding stock by the ladleful making sure you take only the stock, leaving the peas in the pan. Do this until the rice is cooked so the grains are swollen and creamy, but still with a gentle bite. This should take about 20 minutes, but start tasting the rice a few minutes earlier to make sure you don't overcook it into a mush. If you run out of stock simply add some just-boiled water from your kettle.

8. When the rice is just cooked as you like it tip in all the peas, and continue to cook for 30 seconds, still stirring. Turn off the heat, add the parmesan and the rest of the butter, give one final stir and cover the pan with a lid or plate for 2 minutes to let the dish settle.

9. Serve in bowls with extra shavings of parmesan and parsley scattered over the top. This is great with a simple watercress and tomato salad.

MORE THAN 40 PER CENT OF THE WORLD'S POPULATION LIVE IN LOW-INCOME COUNTRIES – YET THESE COUNTRIES ACCOUNT FOR JUST THREE PER CENT OF WORLD TRADE.

Christine Hayes
Sort-of Irish Stew

This is an adapted recipe from my Irish family. Once you've opened the bottle of Fairtrade Cabernet Syrah, **it's very easy to finish the bottle...**

Serves 2

rack of lamb (around 6 cutlets)
3–4 shallots, chopped
1 clove garlic, finely chopped
1 ½ cups lamb or vegetable stock
2 handfuls tiny new potatoes
8 small whole baby carrots
2–3 sprigs rosemary, finely chopped
a good slug of Co-op Fairtrade Chilean Cabernet Syrah
salt and freshly ground black pepper

1. Brown the rack of lamb for 3 minutes on each side in a hot ridged frying pan.
2. Remove from pan and chuck in the shallots and garlic for 1 minute, then remove.
3. Pour hot stock into a saucepan and add potatoes, carrots, the garlic and shallots, rosemary and seasoning. Bring to the boil.
4. Place the rack of lamb on top of everything, turn down the heat and cover the saucepan. Simmer for 15 minutes for rare, 20 minutes for medium rare.
5. Remove the rack of lamb and the vegetables, using a slotted spoon, into a shallow casserole dish, cover and leave to rest for 5 minutes.
6. Reduce the liquid in the pan a little by putting it on a high heat for 2–3 minutes.
7. Add a good slug of red wine, leave on a high heat for another 2 minutes, then take off heat and cover with a lid to keep hot.
8. Slice the lamb into six cutlets, place three on each plate, and spoon on spuds and carrots around it. Add the red wine sauce.
9. Serve with buttered, wilted white cabbage sprinkled with thyme. (Finely chop a quarter of a head of white cabbage, simmer over a very lower heat with two knobs butter for ten minutes, adding a little of the gravy. Add thyme 2 minutes before removing from heat.)

Jim Allen

Margaret Atwood
Mother Atwood's Molasses Cookies

Sven Arnstein

*In memory of my **grandmother**, Mrs. Florence McGowan Atwood, of Nova Scotia, Canada.*

¹/₂ cup Fairtrade sugar
¹/₃ cup shortening
¹/₂ teaspoon salt
1 teaspoon ground ginger
1 cup molasses
1 teaspoon bicarbonate of soda,
**   dissolved in ¹/₄ cup hot water**
3 cups of white flour, plus flour for rolling

1. Cream the sugar and shortening together in a bowl.
2. Add the salt, ginger and molasses, and mix well. Add the bicarbonate of soda and then the flour. Mix and knead well into a dough.
3. Roll out the dough and cut out with a cookie cutter. Place the circles on a greased baking tray.
4. Bake the cookies at Gas Mark 4/180°C/350°F for 8– 9 minutes. Place them on a wire rack to cool.

Donna Air
Poppet's Special Porridge

*This is a recipe both my daughter and I really enjoy. I know she is getting a really **nutritious** start to the day and it is very tasty too.*

small dash of water
apples, raisins or alternative fruit
a stick of cinnamon

Put all the ingredients in a pan and simmer for five minutes. Mix the fruit and juice with cooked oats. Add maple syrup or cream to taste.

Jim Marks

Jeni Barnett
My Chicken Soup

My family came from poverty. When the Jews got elbowed out of Russia, my mob climbed on the nearest boat with their hopes tied in string bags along with their memories. My grandmother made chicken soup for everybody in her tenement block, handing out bowls of **Jewish penicillin** *as the fascists marched through Cable Street. This recipe was passed down to me; I've added my 21st-century twist. Every Jewish mother swears that her recipe is the best and I am no exception. This simple broth is my offering to help those of us who can only dream of a good nourishing meal and a sincere plea that we do indeed make poverty history.*

Will feed lots of gentiles and a few Jews…

1 whole chicken, with giblets if you have them
1 big onion
1 big carrot
2 celery stalks plus leaves
1 big squashy tomato
1 bunch of parsley
3 cloves of garlic (more if you're feeling poorly)
1 lump of ginger
salt and white pepper

1. Bung the whole chicken in a big saucepan and cover it with clean, clear water. When it comes to the boil 'shar' (my bubba's word) off the scum, refill with clean water and continue to spoon off all the scum.

2. Now add all the vegetables including the parsley, garlic and ginger; only the celery needs to be cut in half, leave the rest of the vegetation whole. Now bring the soup back to the boil, season with enough salt and white pepper, then put it on the back burner, on the lowest light, for a minimum of three hours.

3. When mouthwatering aromas fill your kitchen turn off the heat. When it's cool enough to handle strain the liquid into one container, put the mushy vegetables into another and the chicken into a third.

4. Eat as a clear broth, or with the shredded chicken or the soft vegetables, or even with some kneidles (matzo-meal dumplings) or indeed lokschen (vermicelli). Refrigerate the remaining soup and when it's cold remove the schmaltz from the top. Yes, now you know what schmaltz means; yes, it's fat, marvellous spread on rye bread or for cooking.

Enough already, now eat and be well.

POOR COUNTRIES LOSE AROUND $100 BILLION A YEAR – TWICE AS MUCH AS THEY GET IN AID – BECAUSE RICH COUNTRIES PUT UP BARRIERS THAT PREVENT THEM MAKING THE MOST OUT OF TRADE.

I first came across this recipe for goat kebabs whilst on the trail of Fairtrade coffee in **Rwanda**, so it's very close to my heart. So why was I on the trail of coffee? People are always telling me that I should buy Fairtrade coffee and my question is WHY? I want to drink coffee, with a clear conscience but it has to taste really good too. So I set off on the trail of a Fairtrade coffee, on a journey that takes me to Rwanda, the small country in central Africa. In 1994 it was the scene of a terrible genocide that claimed around one million lives.

My destination is the small village of Kizi. On the slopes, above the village, farmers grow coffee – fine quality Arabica coffee bushes producing the best beans at high altitude. Here the farmers have formed the Abahuzamugambi cooperative, whose name translates as **'those who have common goals'**.

In the past, farmers were on their own, washing the coffee cherries and drying the beans outside their own small homesteads. Small wonder that they were not able to access the

Oz Clarke

Goat Kebabs & Chips

quality coffee market, and their coffee was sold for a pittance on the **world market**. Today all that has changed: new businesses have opened (residents of Kizi are proud to tell me they have Rwanda's first ever rural bank!) and the premium from Fairtrade sales funds the local school.

And what does the coffee taste like … As they say in Kigali *Biraryoshe* (delicious)! And I am drinking it with a **clear conscience**.

The kebabs and chips should be accompanied with banana beer or *urgwagwa* as it is called in Rwanda. There, the beer is in a clay pot and passed around, with everyone drinking from the one reed straw.

FOR THE KEBABS

leg of goat cut into bite-size pieces
    chilli sauce (Spanish, Portuguese
    or West Indian)

FOR THE CHIPS
good quality potatoes like Maris Piper
oil for deep-frying
freshly ground sea salt

1. Marinate the goat meat in the chilli sauce for several hours.
2. Peel and cut the potato into chips.
3. Thread the meat on to skewers.
4. Prepare the outdoor barbeque in the normal way (or the grill indoors if you don't have an outdoor barbeque).
5. Deep-fry the chips until golden and crispy.
6. When the barbecue or grill is hot, throw on the skewered meat and cook, turning midway, until charred outside and tender inside.
7. Place the cooked chips on kitchen towel to mop up the excess fat. Sprinkle them with sea salt and serve with the kebabs.

Over 1 billion people –
most of them farmers
and farm workers – live
on $1 or less a day.

Jamelia - singer

a taste of the east

Tom Norrington Davies

Lottie Davies

As someone who makes a living by being obsessed with good food, it is an honour to be part of a project like this. It comes as a timely reminder that food is meant to be about **nurturing and sharing** in the age of scares, shortages, scandalous exploitation and the toll that massive commercialism has taken on our environment. Too often these days it is easy for the consumer to feel both bewildered and helpless to affect any changes to all the above. This need not be the case. The release of the third Band Aid single last Christmas and the worldwide response to the tsunami of Boxing Day showed me that we are capable of sharing our wealth and **good fortune**. Actually we could be doing this every time we go shopping for the things we take for granted. Take tea for example. The average person in Britain drinks 3.5 cups per day. By switching to Fairtrade tea you are making a difference to the people that grow and sell this commodity. At the moment you have to search for the Fairtrade versions of goods such as tea and coffee amongst a mountain of the cheaper stuff. But it is hardly like

looking for a needle in a haystack. Nor is it expensive in any real sense. And if we all start to demand that companies with **buying power** like the bigger supermarkets stock exclusively Fairtrade goods where they are available, and stop obsessing over driving down prices, then who knows? We could really be making a difference. I hope you enjoy this simple recipe which I have chosen to show that there is so much more to tea than the average cuppa.

Hot smoking fish over a perfumed tea is popular in the Far East. It caught on here where it is sometimes described as tea smoking, which I think is a little disingenuous. If the tea is too hot the smoke kills the delicate fragrance of the tea and the marinade. This is a dish best made at a moderate pace in a moderate oven. You could improvise a smoker by using a bamboo steamer or the grilling tray of your oven and tin foil. It is not a messy process. It will also work with various fish. In the season, I love to use sea trout or salmon, but you could just as easily use river trout or a chunky white fish like cod and pollock.

Tea-roasted Sea Trout, Watercress & Green Bean Salad

Serves 4

3 tablespoons soy sauce

5 tablespoons shaoxing wine (or sherry)

1 tablespoon Fairtrade runny honey

3 or 4 thin slices root ginger

2 spring onions, chopped, keeping white and green parts separate

4 x 200 g fillets wild seat trout or salmon, scaled and de-boned

200 g basmati or jasmine rice

4 tablespoons Fairtrade loose leaf tea of your choice (I love lapsang souchong)

FOR THE SALAD

200 g dwarf or bobby beans, topped and tailed

1 Fairtrade avocado pear, sliced roughly

75 g (1 or 2 bunches) watercress, picked and washed

2 tablespoons extra virgin olive oil

$1/2$ teaspoon flaked sea salt

1 level teaspoon cracked peppercorns

1. Combine the soy, wine, honey and ginger with the white part of the spring onions. Pour this over the fish fillets and leave them for as long as possible – overnight is ideal but a couple of hours will do the trick.

2. Preheat the oven to Gas Mark 6/200°C.

3. In a dry pan, heat the rice and tea until you can smell a nutty, roasting smell. Remove from the heat. Line the base of a bamboo steamer or grilling tray with tin foil and pour the rice mix into it. Now lay the fish in the next level of the steamer (or on the rack over the grill tray). Cover the fish tightly with more foil and then with the steamer lid or foil. Place in the oven for 45 minutes. Remove it and rest it for at least 15 more minutes before uncovering it and serving.

4. In the meantime make the salad. Blanch the beans in plenty of boiling salted water until they are just tender. Allow them to cool and toss them with the slices of avocado, the watercress, the greens of the spring onions, the olive oil, salt and crushed peppercorns.

5. Serve the salad and the fish with wholemeal bread and butter.

Produce Covered
by the FAIRTRADE Mark

Thanks to **consumer** support, Fairtrade products are now no longer niche but mainstream products that are available in major supermarkets. Check out your local shops and supermarkets for the following products:

Cocoa, coffee, tea, chocolate, honey, jam and marmalade, chutney, mangoes, juices, rice, sugar, wine, beers, apples, plums, pears, pineapples, avocados, bananas, oranges, lemons, satsumas, clementines, coconuts, green and red grapes, nuts and nut oil, cereal bars, muesli, biscuits, cakes and snacks.

Many high street coffee shops also sell Fairtrade coffee, tea and other products.There is also a wide choice of organic coffee, tea, bananas and some other fruits, honey, cocoa and chocolate products carrying the FAIRTRADE Mark and the range is increasing steadily.

Quite a lot of the fruit (apples, pears, plums, citrus, grapes) is seasonal (peak period tends to be between December and May/June when our local produce in Britain is out of season). There's also a growing number of catering suppliers who can help you get Fairtrade products into your school, college or workplace. You can find all the latest product information at www.fairtrade.org.uk

Cashew, Prawn, Brazil Nut & Lemon Rice

Jonny Ring

Vicky Bhogal

This is a special variation of a dish that is becoming rather famous indeed. It is so unbelievably simple, easy to make and healthy, yet the taste belies all these qualities. For me, it not only functions as the perfect luxurious accompaniment for a dinner party but also as a great, risotto-style, bowl of comfort food, served with a lashing of natural yogurt, that is just as **virtuous as it is heartwarming**. *You just put everything in the pan together, quickly stir fry, add water, steam and, Bob's your Uncleji, there you have it. If you want to be a little indulgent, treat yourself to a Bombayllini too.*

Serves 2

2 tablespoons mild and light olive oil
1 teaspoon cumin seeds
$\frac{1}{2}$ onion thinly sliced
zest of 1 Fairtrade lemon
250 g cooked and peeled prawns
2 tomatoes, diced
handful of chopped coriander
$\frac{1}{2}$ cup/60 g (2 oz) cashew nuts
$\frac{1}{2}$ cup/60 g (2 oz) chopped toasted Fairtrade
    brazil nuts
1 teaspoon dried red chilli flakes
$\frac{1}{2}$ teaspoon salt
$\frac{1}{2}$ cup/110 g (4 oz) basmati rice, washed until
    the water runs clear
1 cup/125 ml (4 fl oz) water

1. Heat the oil in a pan and add the cumin seeds. When sizzling, add the onion and lemon zest and fry until the onion is translucent.
2. Add the prawns, tomatoes, coriander, cashews, brazils, chilli and salt and stir fry for 30 seconds.
3. Add the rice and stir fry for a further 30 seconds.
4. Add the water and bring to the boil. Turn the heat down very low, cover and steam for 15 minutes.
5. Graze gently with a fork to loosen the grains, then serve.

Bombayllinis

Based on the Bellini, this Fairtrade version adds an exotic charm to the glitzy tipple, perfect for a dinner party.

Serves 8–10

juice of a Fairtrade lemon
$1/2$ cup/125 g (4 $1/2$ oz) of Fairtrade sugar
1 large Fairtrade mango, peeled and stoned
1 bottle of champagne or sparkling non-alcoholic spritzer
slivers of Fairtrade mango and very thin slices of Fairtrade orange to garnish

1. Dip the rims of the champagne glasses into a saucer of the lemon juice.
2. Dip them straight away into the sugar, for a frosted effect.
3. Purée the mango in a blender.
4. Divide the purée amongst champagne glasses, and top with champagne. You need roughly a third mango puree to two-thirds champagne.
5. Garnish with a sliver of mango and a slice of orange.

Our members have greatly benefited from the profits Fairtrade has generated. On top of that, we are now getting technical and financial support that enables us to continue our tradition of excellence. Therefore, Fairtrade membership is very important to our organization and its members.

Tadesse Meskela, General Manager, Oromia Coffee Farmers' Co-operative Union, Ethiopia

Oxfam – Make Trade Fair

Make Trade Fair aims to change world trade rules so that trade can make a real difference in the fight against global poverty. Oxfam's Make Trade Fair campaign is calling on governments, institutions, and multinational companies to change the rules so that trade can become part of the solution to poverty, not part of the problem. Oxfam is calling for:

- Rich countries to remove barriers to imports for all low-income countries.

- A comprehensive ban on agricultural export subsidies, which would end the cycle of over-production and export dumping by rich countries.

- An end to the practice of attaching conditions to IMF-World Bank loans, which force poor countries to open their markets regardless of the impact on poor people.

- Action to stabilise prices for primary commodities at higher levels, and pay more to small farmers.

- Fair patent rules which ensure that poor countries are able to afford new technologies and basic medicines, and that farmers are able to save, exchange, and sell seeds.

- Better employment standards, especially for women.

- A more democratic World Trade Organisation which gives poor countries a stronger voice.

The Oxfam Big Noise Petition
The Big Noise represents the voices of people around the world who are calling for key decision-makers to make trade fair. With your help, Oxfam want to make it the biggest petition ever, make leaders listen, and to make trade fair.

The petition is growing every day and recently went through the 5 million mark. Check out www.maketradefair.com

Bob Judges

Mary Berry
Five Spice Mango Chicken

Perfect to serve cold for a buffet or cooking for numbers – light and **fresh**. Can be made a day ahead and kept in the fridge, this gives time for the flavours to really **infuse** into the chicken.

Serves 8–10

2 large Fairtrade mangoes, roughly chopped
8 mild Peppadew peppers from a jar
6 tablespoons mango chutney
1 x 200 ml carton Greek yogurt
1 tablespoon Chinese five spice powder
juice of 1 Fairtrade lemon
a few drops of Tabasco.
750 g (1 ¾ lb) fresh cooked chicken meat without
    bone
salt and freshly ground black pepper

TO GARNISH
fresh salad leaves
2 mild peppadew peppers, sliced thinly
fresh parsley, chopped

1. Cut the mango flesh from one mango into pieces and put into a food processor. Add rest of the ingredients, except the chicken and whiz until smooth and blended. Season with salt and pepper.
2. Cut the chicken into neat pieces and mix with the mango sauce in a mixing bowl. Cut the remaining mango into 1 cm pieces and mix in with the chicken mixture. Taste and check seasoning.
3. Arrange the salad leaves on a large platter. Spoon the chicken mixture on top and sprinkle over peppadew slices and parsley. Serve cold.

NOTES: If you want to make this a day ahead omit the chopped mango and leave it mixed with a little lemon juice in a bowl in the fridge. Just stir in before serving.

Lulu Grimes
Tea-Smoked Ribs

Use a Fairtrade tea to make this recipe; any loose leaf black tea will do the trick, though if you would like a more **distinct flavour** *choose a Lapsang Souchong. As would be expected, this does create smoke.*

Serves 4

6 tablespoons Fairtrade loose leaf black tea
2 teaspoons cracked black pepper
4 star anise, lightly pounded
2 cardamoms, lightly crushed
1 ½ kg pork ribs, cut across the bone into short
   lengths (ask your butcher to do this)
8 tablespoons Fairtrade honey
2 cloves garlic, crushed
6 tablespoons soy sauce

1. Heat the oven to Gas Mark 4/180°C/fan oven 160°C. Put the tea, pepper, star anise and cardamoms in the bottom of a roasting tin and set a rack on top. The rack shouldn't touch the tea or spices. Put the ribs on top and cover the whole thing with foil. Bake for 40 minutes.
2. Mix the honey, garlic and soy together. Take the ribs out of the oven and take off the foil. Paint the soy mixture over the ribs and put them back in the oven for 40 minutes or until the ribs are tender.

The advantage I see in Fairtrade is that I don't have to use chemicals, which is good for my health, and a healthy environment. It helps to pay the bills and send my children to school; I am getting more for my bananas now.

Regina Joseph, Banana Farmer, Windward Islands Farmers' Association, Dominica

Avial – the Malabar Masterpiece – Exotic Vegetables in a Creamy, Golden Sauce

Pat Chapman

Serves 4 as a sole main course dish with rice

The Malabar coast stretches for hundreds of miles down south western India, from Goa to Cape Cormorin, India's southern most tip. It is known for supremely good vegetable dishes. Avial, known as the 'Malabar masterpiece', mostly contains mixed exotic vegetables, and is perhaps the area's signature dish. The **truly authentic** recipe must contain yoghurt, sour green mango and coconut. Traditional vegetables include all or some of the following: aubergine, plantain, yam, drumstick, pumpkin, snake gourd, karela bitter gourd, ash gourd, spinach, cucumber, carrot and potato. The great Hindu temples of south India prepare Avial at festival time in **vast brass urns**, 5 feet (1.5 metres) high and 10 feet (3 metres) in diameter, to feed the entire local population. This tradition goes back to the time when the temples were built in the 10th century.

675 g (1 ¹/₂ lb) exotic mixed vegetables chosen from the list in recipe intro.
flesh of a fresh Fairtrade coconut and its water
2 garlic cloves
1 or more fresh green chillies, roughly chopped
1 small sour mango, skinned, stoned and chopped
1 teaspoon turmeric
2 tablespoons vegetable oil
2 teaspoons cumin seeds
   100 g (4 oz) natural yoghurt
10 to 12 curry leaves, fresh or dried
salt

TO GARNISH
1 tablespoon sunflower oil
1 teaspoon black mustard seeds
20 curry leaves or fresh coriander leaves
roasted cashew nuts, whole

1. Prepare and trim the vegetables, as appropriate. The tradition is to cut them into thinnish diamond-shaped slices.
2. In the blender, mulch down the coconut, coconut water, garlic, chillies, mango and turmeric, using as little water as necessary to create a pourable paste.
3. Heat the oil and fry the cumin seeds for 10 seconds, then add the paste and continuing stir-frying for about 3 minutes. Turn off the heat.
4. Blanch the vegetables for 3–4 minutes in plenty of water then strain, leaving just enough blanching water to cover the vegetables. Bring back to the simmer.
5. Add the yoghurt, curry leaves and the paste from stage 3 above. The mixture should not be too thick. Simmer for a short while until the vegetables are ready. Salt to taste. Place into a serving bowl.
6. For the garnish, heat the oil in a pan and add mustard seeds and curry or coriander leaves and stir-fry for a couple of minutes. Add the nuts and when hot, pour the garnish onto the Avial in its serving bowl. Serve with boiled rice.

I think that Fairtrade brings security. I know that if I sell to a Fairtrade buyer that I'll get fair treatment. I'm sure that the buyer will be monitored and will buy at a fair price.

Alberto, Sugar Cane Farmer, Costa Rica

The **Fairtrade Foundation**

This is the organisation behind the FAIRTRADE Mark that appears on the products you buy. The Fairtrade Foundation is not a company but a **non-profit organisation** that certifies and promotes Fairtrade and is the UK member of FLO – Fairtrade Labelling Organisation International.

The Fairtrade Foundation was set up in the 1992 by CAFOD, Christian Aid, Oxfam, New Consumer, Traidcraft Exchange, the World Development Movement, and the National Federation of Women's Institutes. They were later joined by several other organisations. With its partners, the Fairtrade Foundation maintains standards by regularly auditing suppliers, and checking contracts and trade terms. It awards the FAIRTRADE Mark to products that meet international Fairtrade standards, as well as its use in promotion and **awareness** raising initiatives.

Each year in March, Fairtrade Fortnight takes place, when local groups across the country link up with supermarkets, wholefood shops, churches, schools and the media to **promote** Fairtrade. Indeed there are now Fairtrade towns and cities and even universities!

Geeta Samtani

This particular recipe for Mango Kadookas is typical of Sindhi cuisine. Sindhis are a very entrepreneurial and outgoing community and their food is influenced by the **Mughals** who passed through the Indus Valley in the region of Sindh. Pickling or making aachars (pickle in Hindi) is a family tradition where especially women (family and friends) would gather together once a year during mango season and make huge quantities of pickles to last the household at least a year. It was something that everyone would really look forward to as a gathering and **family affair**. Every household in India has their own special recipes for various types of pickles. Now times have changed as women now form a significant portion of the workforce and hence this activity is not practised as before.

FOR THE MANGO RELISH (MANGO KADOOKAS)

1 kg raw green mangoes, grated
3–4 tablespoons salt
750 g Fairtrade white sugar
$1/2$–1 teaspoon red chilli powder
1 teaspoon paprika
1 teaspoon onion (nigella) seeds
1–2 teaspoons fennel seeds, crushed
1–2 teaspoons fenugreek seeds, crushed
2–3 cardamoms, crushed
2–3 bay leaves
10–12 black peppercorns
1 stick of cinnamon
3–4 tablespoons white malt vinegar
4–5 cloves of garlic, cut in fine slivers
2–3 cloves

PREPARING THE MANGOES

Please ensure that you purchase raw, green mangoes. Peel and grate. Add the salt and leave for half an hour. Squeeze out all the water.

1. Mix all the ingredients together and leave for a minimum of 3–4 days to mature in a jar. This relish tastes better if it is left to mature for 7–10 days.
2. Check seasoning – add salt and additional red chilli powder for a hotter taste.

This can keep in the fridge for a few months.

Mango Kadookas (Mango Relish) with Keema Tikkis

FOR THE KEEMA TIKKI

Makes 8–10

1 tablespoon oil
3–4 cloves of garlic
1 inch piece of ginger
2 green chillies (optional)
1 medium onion, chopped
500 g minced lamb
1 small tomato, chopped
1 medium potato, chopped in small cubes
salt to taste
$\frac{1}{2}$ teaspoon black cumin seeds
5–6 green cardamoms (crushed)
$\frac{1}{2}$ teaspoon red chilli powder
10–12 black peppercorns
2 cloves
2–3 bay leaves
1 small stick of cinnamon
1 cup water
2 slices of white bread
2–3 tablespoon chopped coriander leaves
1 tablespoon chopped mint leaves
oil for frying

1. Heat the oil in a heavy bottomed pan. Add garlic, ginger, chillies and onion and sauté. Add the minced lamb, tomato, potato, salt and all the spices except the coriander and mint leaves.
2. Add the water and leave to simmer for 10–15 minutes. Then put on high heat and stir fry until the mince is cooked and the liquid has evaporated from the sides of the pan.
3. Remove the bay leaves and cinnamon stick.
4. Soak the bread slices in water and then squeeze all the water out. Add the wet bread to the mince mixture and then put it in the food processor and blitz on pulse a few times, until it is all mixed through.
5. Remove the mixture from the food processor and check the seasoning. Add the chopped coriander and mint leaves.
6. Grease your hands and make small rounds in the shape of a patty. Shallow fry the patties in a non-stick pan and serve with the mango relish.

Paul Merrett
Hot & Sour Broth

*I was born in Zanzibar, East Africa and have often used lots of cooking ideas gleaned from there so its about time I put something back in! I love this – simple preparation and a huge flavour. The trick is in the balancing of **sweet, hot and sour**. Once you've mastered the broth there are many variations to try – meat, fish or my favourite – shellfish. I've used this both in the restaurant and at home.*

Serves 4 starter size portions

2 large red chillies, the smaller the chilli variety the hotter the flavour
1 stick lemongrass, cut roughly
10 coriander leaves
3 tablespoons grated palm sugar
6 lime leaves, these freeze well so buy a bundle
2 limes
Thai fish sauce, to taste
protein of your choice, I like to use fresh tiger prawns, squid rings and scallops

TO MAKE A DECENT CHICKEN STOCK

1 litre of water
stock cube
1 clove of garlic
1 shallot, peeled and roughly cut
4 raw chicken legs

1. Make the stock. Simmer the water and whisk in the stock cube. Add the other ingredients and simmer until the chicken is cooked. Strain and keep only the stock (the chicken legs provide a separate meal or could be flaked in to the finished broth).
2. In a pestle and mortar pound the first five ingredients to a rough paste, the bits should still be definable.
3. Add the juice of the limes and the fish sauce to the mixture.
4. Add the mixture to the stock and stir. Now add your chosen protein.
5. Cook on for 2 minutes and then serve in deep bowls.

Keith Floyd
Thai Fishcakes with Sweet Chilli Sauce

*These are a complete change from your normal fishcake. For a start there is no potato bulking them out, so what you get are the **flavours** from all the individual ingredients. This makes them rather special.*

500 g (1 lb 2oz) raw crab, lobster or prawns, chopped
200 g (7 oz) skinned boneless white fish, chopped
2 tablespoons Thai red or green curry paste
1 egg, beaten
1 tablespoon finely chopped fresh coriander
a couple of dashes of fish sauce
1 teaspoon baking powder
2 fresh green chillies, finely chopped
1 tablespoon brown sugar
3 or 4 garlic cloves, peeled and crushed
2 fresh or dried Kaffir lime leaves, very finely chopped
75 g (3 oz) frozen petit pois
plain flour for dusting
vegetable oil for deep frying

FOR THE SWEET CHILLI SAUCE
10 fresh green chillies, deseeded and chopped
4 garlic cloves, peeled
1 tablespoon fish sauce
juice of two limes
2 shallots, peeled
1 tablespoon Fairtrade runny honey

1. Make the sweet chilli sauce. Briefly whiz all the ingredients in a food processor – not too finely so you can still make out the ingredients. Spoon into a bowl.
2. Coarsely purée the seafood and fish in a food processor, then mix the processed fish with all the other ingredients except the flour and vegetable oil.
3. Form the mixture into small bite-sized cakes and dust them in the flour.
4. Heat the oil in a large pan and deep-fry the fishcakes until golden
5. Serve with sweet chilli sauce.

Ken Hom
Beef with Ginger & Pineapple

*This recipe is derived from the original I enjoyed at Lai Ching Heen, the marvellous Chinese restaurant in Hong Kong's Regent Hotel. I regard it as **exemplary** of the innovative New Hong Kong Cuisine in which new ingredients and techniques are being employed to transform traditional recipes.*

Serves 4–6

1 lb (450 g) lean beef steak
1 teaspoon salt
4 teaspoons Chinese rice wine or dry sherry
4 teaspoons sesame oil
1¹/₂ teaspoons cornflour
8 oz (225 g) fresh Fairtrade pineapple
2 red peppers
2 spring onions
2 tablespoons (30 ml) groundnut oil
2 tablespoons shredded fresh root ginger
1 tablespoon (15 ml) water
1 teaspoon light soy sauce

1. Cut the beef into thick ¹/₂ inch x 2 inch (0.5 x 5 cm) slices and put them in a bowl. Add the salt, 2 teaspoons of the rice wine or dry sherry, 2 teaspoons of the sesame oil and the cornflour and mix well.

2. Peel the pineapple and cut into thick slices, discarding the tough core. De-seed the peppers and cut them into wedges. Cut the spring onions into 3 inch (7.5 cm) lengths.

3. Heat the wok, then pour in the groundnut oil. Add the beef and stir fry for 1 minute to brown. Remove the beef with a slotted spoon and set aside.

4. Add the ginger, peppers and spring onions to the wok and stir fry for 1 minute. Pour in the water, the remaining 2 teaspoons of rice wine or sherry and soy sauce and cook for 3 minutes. Drain the juices from the beef into the wok and also add the pineapple. Return the beef to the wok and cook until it and the pineapple are heated through. Add the remaining 2 teaspoons sesame oil and give the mixture one or two final stirs. Serve at once.

IN AFRICA ALONE, A ONE
PER CENT INCREASE IN
THE SHARE OF WORLD
TRADE WOULD GENERATE
$70 BILLION – FIVE TIMES
WHAT THE CONTINENT
GETS IN AID.

5 million farmers and their families are facing ruin because the US governments subsidises its corn farmers to over-produce and dump the surplus at rock-bottom prices in Mexico.

Antonio Banderas - actor

posh nosh

Stephen Shepherd

Matthew Fort
Tonno di Coniglio

*I ate this at Cascina Martini, a restaurant of the highest quality, and it is so typical of the cooking of Monferrato. Tonno di Coniglio is the inland version of tuna in oil. It expressed the **ingenuity** of agricultural communities far from the sea. Fresh sea fish would have been unobtainable, tinned tuna expensive. Rabbit, on the other hand, was relatively inexpensive and readily available. The rabbit had been poached until **tender**, taken off the bone, and then marinated in olive oil, a little garlic, parsley and thyme. The meat had taken on that particular firm, flaky texture of tuna, and had absorbed the herbs and garlic, too.*

1 rabbit
20–30 sage leaves
20 cloves garlic, unpeeled
1 litre extra virgin olive oil
salt and pepper

1. Cut the rabbit up into pieces. Put in a pan and cover with salted water. Bring to simmer and cook gently until the meat is ready to fall off the bones, about 45 minutes. Drain the rabbit. Pull the flesh off the bones while still warm.

2. Put the meat into an earthenware container in layers, with a layer of sage leaves and garlic cloves between each, seasoning each layer as you build. You should have at least three layers of rabbit. Cover with oil.

3. Put in the fridge and leave for at least a night, preferably two or three.

4. At the Cascina Martini, it was served on a bed of rice, another local ingredient, but slightly bitter chicory leaves do very well.

Mitchell Tonks
Zuppa de Pescatore

*I first cooked this dish after being inspired by a picture I had seen in a cookbook a few years earlier. It looked fantastic and so appetising seeing a pan packed full of colour with all different kinds of seafood. I imagined the dish in the picture was exactly how **local fishermen** on small Mediterranean ports would eat it. I have since cooked it on a beach over a wood fire, on a family sailing holiday. I had no fish stock so I made do with seawater and wild herbs. It was great sitting round diving into the pan and spooning out the fresh cooked fish and shellfish. It can be as simple as this to make a meal become part of **your memories.** Any selection of fish and shellfish can be used – lobster, clams, mussels, chunks of skate, steaks of hake, gurnard and cod, the choice is yours; buy enough to fill the pan packed tightly in one layer.*

Serves 4

1 shallot, finely chopped
2 cloves of garlic, chopped
olive oil
2 roasted tomatoes
pinch of saffron
3 or 4 sprigs of thyme
splash of Pernod
selection of fish
570 ml (1 pint) fish stock
sea salt
parsley or basil, chopped, for sprinkling over
   the top
grilled bread
aioli

1. In a large pan, sweat the shallots and garlic in the olive oil.
2. Add the tomatoes, saffron and thyme and stir together.
3. Add the Pernod and tip the pan away from you allowing it to catch fire and burn off the alcohol.
4. Add the fish and cover with the fish stock. Simmer for 8–10 minutes.
5. Remove the thyme and season. Finally, sprinkle with fresh chopped herbs and accompany with grilled bread topped with the rich, garlicky aioli.

AIOLI

Rich mayonnaise made with thick green olive oil, heavily flavoured with garlic. It is perfect on a croûton to top Zuppa de Pescatore or other fish stews. And I always have a bowl on the table when eating steamed clams or mussels. Crisp-fried goujons of sole also benefit from being dunked in aioli.

2 egg yolks
1 teaspoon Dijon mustard
4 cloves of garlic, crushed into a paste
150 ml/5 fl oz good olive oil
juice of ½ lemon
sea salt

1. Put the egg yolks in a bowl with the mustard and garlic. Whilst whisking add the olive oil in a steady stream until a thick emulsion is formed. Add the lemon juice, season, and let it stand for an hour before serving.

Ben O'Donoghue

Ben's Curried Crab

It seems such a simple thing to contribute a recipe that will give a few people **pleasure** yet hopefully bring some the freedom from poverty. It's an honour to be involved in such an admirable cause.

Serves 4–6

1 kg mud crab (however you can use any
  seafood, it's great with fish heads!)
100 g diced tomatoes
10 curry leaves
10 g turmeric
15 g chilli powder
salt
20 ml olive oil
100 ml coconut milk

FOR THE PASTE
200 g white onion
50 g desiccated coconut
20 g coriander seeds
10 g cumin seeds
20 g peppercorns
30 g green chilli
20 g ginger
40 g garlic
150 ml vinegar

1. Kill the crab by placing it in the freezer. Remove the legs and crack the shells with a rolling pin. Remove the top of the shell, clean and chop in half.
2. Purée all the ingredients for the paste with the vinegar.
3. Heat the oil in a pot and sauté the paste over a low heat for 5–10 minutes. Add the rest of the ingredients except the coconut milk and cook for 5 minutes.
4. Add the crab and ¹/₂ cup of water and bring to the boil. Turn down the heat to a simmer and cook for 10 minutes then mix in the coconut milk and cook for 2–3 minutes. Serve with steamed rice.

Piers Fletcher

Helen Fielding

Bridget Jones' recipe for cheese

As Mum and Una are always telling me: **"A good cook is an artist as well as a craftsman, darling."** This recipe for cheese is both arty and crafty as well as being stylish and nutritious.

Serves 1

cheese

1. Take cheese out of fridge.
2. Cut off mould.
3. Eat.

If our grapes sell well in Britain we will get a Fairtrade premium. This money will be used for community projects such as providing water and starting a brick making factory so we can build schools and clinics. That will give our home communities a double benefit.

Thomas Thebeetsile, Grape Farmer, South Africa

Mourad Mazouz
Couscous Berber with Pan-fried Scallops & Langoustine Red Pepper Coulis

The basis of every society should be to feed their population. When we achieve this we will make progress. Sadly, the downfall of society throughout the ages has been greed and the neglect of our natural environment. Food and love are the most important things in life.

Serves 6

250 g of couscous
2 red peppers
75 ml olive oil
2 cloves of garlic, chopped
120 g of peas
150 g of broad beans
100 g of French beans
2–3 large handfuls fresh coriander
24 medium size scallops
18 langoustines
salt and freshly ground black pepper

1. Prepare the couscous according to the instructions on the package and keep warm.
2. Cut the peppers into big pieces and pulp them in the liquidizer to make the coulis.
3. Heat 2 teaspoons of olive oil in a pan; add the garlic, the blended peppers and a glass of water. Reduce to half and pass the mixture through a chinois (or sieve). Keep warm.
4. Cook the peas, broad beans and French beans in salted water for 5 minutes.
5. In a large bowl, mix the couscous with the green vegetables, chopped coriander and 2 teaspoons of oil to make a paste.
6. Put 2 teaspoons of olive oil in a non-stick pan. When hot, put the scallops in the pan and cook each side for a minute. Remove them from the pan.
7. Sprinkle salt and pepper on the langoustines, and cook them in hot oil for a minute on each side.
8. In the middle of a plate, make a dome-like shape with the couscous paste. Pour the pepper coulis around the dome and place the seafood on the sauce.

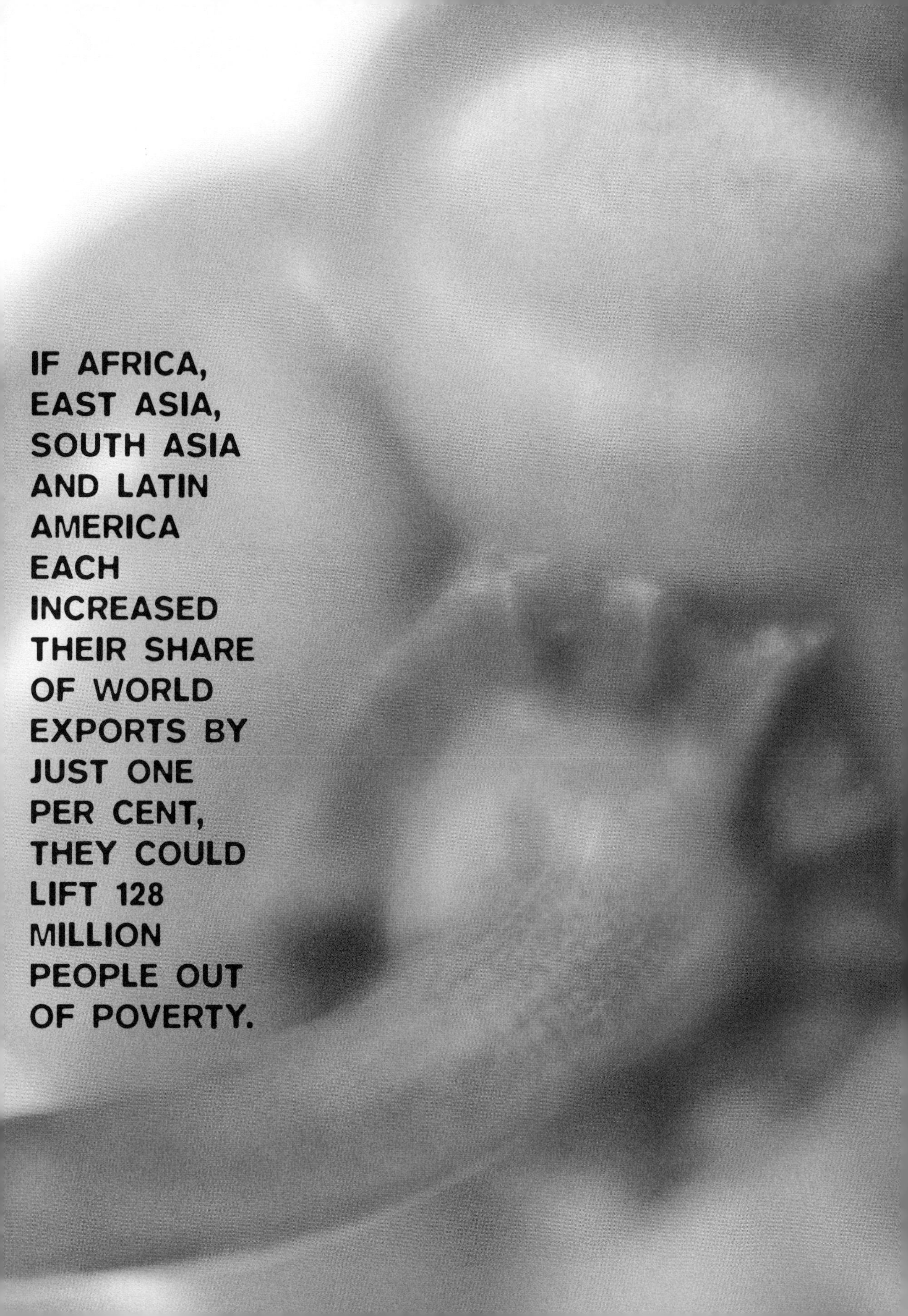

IF AFRICA,
EAST ASIA,
SOUTH ASIA
AND LATIN
AMERICA
EACH
INCREASED
THEIR SHARE
OF WORLD
EXPORTS BY
JUST ONE
PER CENT,
THEY COULD
LIFT 128
MILLION
PEOPLE OUT
OF POVERTY.

Iqbal Wahhab &
Vivek Singh

*Together with our Halibut with Coconut and Ginger Sauce, this could claim to be The Cinnamon Club's signature dish, and is certainly one of the most popular choices on our menu. Vivek created it with a bottle of wine in his hand. He and our wine buyer, Laurent Chaniac, were trying to **devise a recipe** to go with a St Joseph Les Pierres Sèches Domaine Combier 1997. Inventing a dish to suit a wine is not **the usual way** of doing things and it caused quite a stir when we first opened – but it worked. In the restaurant, we serve this with Wild Mushroom and Spinach Stir-fry. A Californian Pinot Noir will go just as well with this spectacular duck dish.*

Serves 4

4 duck breasts, preferably Gressingham duck
1 tablespoon vegetable or corn oil

FOR THE MARINADE
1 tablespoon vegetable or corn oil
1 teaspoon salt
1 teaspoon red chilli powder

FOR THE SESAME TAMARIND SAUCE
1 tablespoon sesame seeds
1 tablespoon coriander seeds
1 teaspoon cumin seeds
$^1/_2$ teaspoon fenugreek seeds
1 tablespoon desiccated coconut
100 ml (3$^1/_2$ fl oz/scant $^1/_2$ cup) vegetable or
   corn oil
1 tablespoon cashew nuts
1 teaspoon mustard seeds
$^1/_2$ teaspoon black onion seeds
10 fresh curry leaves
1 quantity of boiled onion paste (see below)
2 teaspoons mild red chilli powder
$^1/_2$ teaspoon ground turmeric
50 g (2 oz/$^1/_4$ cup) tamarind paste
up to 150 ml/$^1/_4$ pint/$^2/_3$ cup duck stock or
   water (optional)
1 teaspoon salt
1 tablespoon jaggery or molasses sugar

FOR THE BOILED ONION PASTE

Makes about 300 g (11 oz)

1 large onion, cut into 2.5 cm (1 inch) cubes
250 ml (8 fl oz) water

Seared Duck Breasts with Sesame Tamarind Sauce

1. Make the boiled onion paste. Put the onion and water in a small pan and simmer for 15–20 minutes, until the onion is soft. Purée in a food processor or blender until smooth. The paste will keep for 3 days in the fridge.

2. Mix together all the ingredients for the marinade and rub them over the duck breasts. Set aside for 30 minutes.

3. Make the sauce by mixing together the sesame, coriander, cumin and fenugreek seeds and roasting them in a dry frying pan over a moderate heat until they begin to colour. Set aside.

4. Roast the coconut in the same pan until golden, then add to the seeds.

5. Heat a teaspoon of the oil in the pan, add the cashew nuts and fry until golden. Place in a food processor with the roasted seeds and coconut and blend to a smooth paste with a little water.

6. Heat the remaining oil in a large pan until very hot. Add the mustard seeds, followed by the black onion seeds and curry leaves. Reduce the heat, add the onion paste and cook, stirring, until it thickens. Then stir in the chilli powder, turmeric and tamarind and bring to a simmer. Add the nut and seed paste and cook for 3–4 minutes, until the oil begins to separate out at the side of the pan. It is important to stir constantly, as the sauce has a tendency to stick. If it becomes too thick, add enough duck stock or water to give the consistency of thin cream. Stir in the salt and the jaggery or sugar, remove from the heat and keep warm.

7. Heat the oil in an ovenproof frying pan, add the breasts, skin-side down, and sear until well browned. Turn the breasts over and transfer the pan to an oven preheated to Gas Mark 4/180°C. Roast for 15 minutes; the duck should still be pink inside. Leave to rest for 5 minutes, then slice neatly. Divide the sauce between four serving plates and arrange the duck on top.

Jason Lowe

Mark Hix

Fried Goose Eggs with St George's Mushrooms & Wild Garlic

*St George's mushrooms are the first British mushrooms, along with the rare morel, to pop up. Their arrival time depends on our **temperamental** weather, but they should be available in specialist shops at this time of the year. They have a firm meaty texture similar to that of a flat-cap mushroom without the black spores under the cap. Open cup mushrooms or quartered field mushrooms can be used instead.*

Serves 4

60 g butter
250–300 g St George's mushrooms or flat
  mushrooms
1 tablespoon chopped wild garlic leaves
  (optional)
olive oil or goose or duck fat for frying
4 goose eggs
salt and freshly ground black pepper

1. Melt the butter in a heavy, or non-stick, frying pan, add the mushrooms, season with salt and freshly ground black pepper and gently sauté them on a medium heat for 5–7 minutes until cooked.
2. Add the wild garlic, remove from the heat and keep warm in a low oven.
3. Melt a little olive oil or goose fat in the pan – it must be a good, non-stick one – and crack in the goose eggs one at a time (they are big). If you have more than one pan it helps. Cook on a low heat for 3–4 minutes or longer if you get squeamish at the thought of those overwhelming yolks.
4. Remove the eggs with a fish slice or slide them out straight on to plates and spoon the mushrooms and wild garlic around. This is very filling. If you're having it for brunch it'll do you until dinner.

Manos Chadzikostantis

Tessa Kiros

Prawns with Lemon, Peri Peri, Garlic & Feta

I love the idea of Fairtrade. If everyone puts honesty into their moments then every thing we collect and **make in this world** *will be more special. Everyone who has tasted this dish loves it and still now I use it for a special occasion dinner – it seems very 'celebration'. My mother still salts every single prawn individually; once she has slit and removed the dark line of the prawn she* **sprinkles salt** *along this. You can just scatter salt over each layer in the saucepan. This dish needs very little else – bread, some white rice or couscous and a large green salad.*

Serves 6 or more

2 kg (4 lb 8 oz) large raw prawns (shrimp),
   unpeeled
200 g (7 oz) butter
10 garlic cloves, finely chopped
45 g ($^3/_4$ cup) chopped parsley
less than 1 teaspoon peri peri spice or chilli
   powder
juice of 4 Fairtrade lemons
400 g (14 oz) feta cheese
salt

1. Clean the prawns and cut a slit through the shell down the back from the bottom of the head to the beginning of the tail. Remove the dark vein with the point of a sharp knife. Rinse the prawns under running water and drain well.

2. Dot about 80 g (2 $^3/_4$ oz) of the butter over the base of a large cast-iron casserole dish. Arrange a single layer of prawns in the dish and season with salt. Scatter about a third of the garlic and parsley over the top. Sprinkle with a little of the peri peri.

3. Dot about half of the remaining butter over the top and arrange another layer of prawns, scattered with garlic, parsley and peri peri or chilli powder. Repeat the layer, finishing up the ingredients. Put the lid on, turn the heat to medium-high and cook for about 10 minutes, until the prawns have brightened up a lot and their flesh is white. Add the lemon juice, crumble the feta over the top and rock the dish from side to side to move the sauce about. Spoon some sauce over the prawns. Cover the casserole, lower the heat and cook for another 10 minutes or until the feta has just melted, shaking the pan again. Take the dish straight to the table and give everyone a hot finger bowl with lemon juice to clean their hands afterwards.

Diana Henry

Thyme, Oregano & Citrus Roasted Poussins

A really easy, gloriously aromatic dish that **looks stunning**.

Serves 4

4 poussins
4 Fairtrade oranges, skin left on,
 cut into large wedges
olive oil
a small bunch of flat-leaf parsley
salt and freshly ground black pepper

FOR THE MARINADE
zest of 1 Fairtrade orange and 1 lime
juice of 4 Fairtrade oranges and 1 lime
90 ml/6 tablespoons balsamic vinegar
125 ml (4 fl oz) olive oil
6 garlic cloves, crushed
leaves from about 6 sprigs thyme
45 ml (3 tablespoons) dried Greek oregano
 (rigani)

1. Mix all the marinade ingredients together. Put the poussins, breast side-down, into the marinade, cover and refrigerate for a couple of hours or overnight. Move the poussins around every so often so that all the sides get a chance to soak in the marinade.
2. Preheat to oven to Gas Mark 4/180°C. Take the poussins out of the marinade and put them into a roasting tin with the oranges. Drizzle a little extra olive oil over the oranges and season them. Roast for 50 minutes, spooning the marinade over everything as it cooks.
3. When the poussins are cooked, drain off the pan juices, skim off the fat and slightly reduce the juices in a saucepan by boiling for a few minutes, until you have something with the consistency of light gravy.
4. Serve the poussins surrounded by the orange wedges and parsley leaves, with the juices on the side.

WHEN EXPORTING TO RICH
COUNTRIES, PRODUCERS
IN POOR COUNTRIES PAY
TARIFFS THAT ARE FOUR
TIMES HIGHER THAN THOSE
PAID BY PRODUCERS IN
OTHER RICH COUNTRIES.

India Knight
Osso Bucco

This has always been one of my favourite things to eat: my mother used to make it for me on my **birthday**. Here is a simplified version of her recipe. It is fantastically delicious, low-effort and completely **idiot-proof**, plus it looks and smells fantastic. Please buy the veal from a decent organic butcher (mine is from The Ginger Pig in London W1) and serve with risotto alla Milanese, i.e. risotto to which you have added saffron.

To serve 6, with enough for small seconds

8 good big pieces of veal shin
plain flour
sea salt and ground black pepper
3 rounded tablespoons dried thyme
good olive oil
$^1/_2$ –$^3/_4$ bottle of okay but not amazing dry white wine (depending on the size of your pot)
1 fat bushy twig fresh thyme
6 bay leaves
15 black peppercorns
just over half a 400 g can chopped tomatoes (or 4 fresh chopped tomatoes if it's summer and they actually taste of something)

FOR THE GREMOLATA
1 bunch flat leaf parsley
zest of 3 fat Fairtrade lemons
4 fat cloves of garlic

1. Dredge the pieces of veal in plain flour which you have seasoned generously with salt, ground pepper and 2 tablespoons of dried thyme. Brown briefly in the olive oil. Don't crowd the pan – do it in batches.

2. If you have a huge enough casserole, lay the meat flat in it; if not, put it on its side. Add white wine to barely cover. Throw in the fresh thyme, the remaining tablespoon of dried thyme, the bay leaves, peppercorns and the tomatoes.

3. Simmer for 2 hours, covered, on a very low flame. Check the liquid situation after one hour; if you think there's too much juice (though I feel you can't have too much of a good thing – the juice is made for dipping crusty bread into), take the lid off. Also, push any sticky-outy bits of meat down so they all get a go at being immersed. Nothing will happen if you take a nap by accident and cook this for longer – the idea is for the meat to flake off the bone.

4. Make the gremolata just before you're ready to eat: chop off the parsley roots but don't bother taking the leaves off the stalk. Chop the garlic roughly. Grate the lemon peel carefully (the pith is bitter). Chuck the whole lot in a blender and pulse until coarse, or use a mezzaluna.

5. Scatter the gremolata over the veal. Serve. Swoon with delight, and don't forget to feast on the marrowbones.

Much love has gone into growing this fruit. My passion is to do something, not just for me, but to help other people. I am poor, but I sincerely want to help other people.

German Romero Espinoza,
Mango Grower, Ecuador

The **FAIRTRADE** Mark

Depending on how you look at it, the FAIRTRADE Mark depicts a producer **holding up his arm in cheer** or a landscape with the sun in the sky and a road advancing towards you. Both of these images symbolise the essence of Fairtrade – a way forward to a better life and trade justice for producers and workers across the globe.

The FAIRTRADE Mark is an independent consumer label which appears on UK Fairtrade products as a guarantee that they have given their producers **a better deal**, in accordance to a set of internationally agreed standards that aim to **make a real improvement** in their lives.

The European Union
gives its dairy farmers
$2 a day in subsidies
for every cow. This is
more than half the
world's population have
to live on each day.

Michael Stipe - singer

sweet somethings

Jane Asher
Banana Cake with Peaches & Pears

Ivan Merrill

This wonderful tasting, firm cake is also reasonably 'healthy' and can be served on many different occasions. Leave it plain, dust it with a little icing sugar or perhaps even ice it properly. It would also be delicious spread with a little Crème Anglaise and decorated with pieces of dried fruit.

Serves 12

225 g (¹/₂ lb) butter
225 g (¹/₂ lb) caster sugar
3 eggs
340 g (12 oz) Fairtrade bananas
225 g (¹/₂ lb plain flour
¹/₂ teaspoon salt
¹/₄ teaspoon bicarbonate of soda
3 tablespoons yogurt
85 g (3 oz) dried peaches, coarsely chopped
85 g (3 oz) dried pears, coarsely chopped
butter and flour for cake tin

1. Heat the oven to Gas Mark 4/180°C/350°F. Butter and flour a 20 cm (8 inch) square cake tin.
2. Cream the butter and sugar together in a bowl, then add the eggs, one at a time, beating well.
3. Blend the bananas and whisk into the mixture in the bowl.
4. Sift the dry ingredients (flour, salt and bicarbonate of soda) and fold in with a metal spoon.
5. Add the yoghurt and the chopped dried fruits and fold in well. Pour the mixture into the cake and bake in the preheated oven for 1 hour, or until a skewer comes out clean when inserted.
6. Leave the cake to cool in the tin for 10 minutes, then run a knife around the edge and turn the cake out onto a rack to cool completely before serving.

Brian Turner CBE
Coffee & Cream Bread & Butter Pudding

An opportunity to help those less fortunate than ourselves is always welcome but when they are people who provide us with a product like coffee that gives us pleasure it's doubly so.

Serves 4

$^1/_4$ **pint milk**
$^3/_4$ **pint double cream**
1 espresso cup of strong Fairtrade coffee
1 vanilla pod
2 eggs
5 egg yolks
2 oz unrefined caster sugar
6 x 1-day-old croissants
4 oz unsalted butter
6 oz Californian raisins

FOR THE TOPPING
$^1/_4$ **pint whipped cream**
2 oz grated dark Fairtrade chocolate
icing sugar to dust

1. Put the milk, double cream, coffee and opened vanilla pod into a saucepan and bring to the boil.
2. Whisk the eggs, yolks and caster sugar together. Slice the croissants in half lengthwise. Use 1 oz butter to grease an ovenproof dish.
3. Using the remaining butter, spread this on the cut sides of the croissants. Lay half of them on the base of the dish, butter side up. Sprinkle with raisins and lay the remaining croissants on top
4. Let the boiled cream cool a little and pour it on to the egg mixture stirring all the time. Put back on to the heat and stir until it starts to thicken, and then take it off immediately.
5. Strain half of the cream mixture over the croissants and allow to soak in for 15 minutes, gradually straining over the rest of the mixture until all is in the dish. Preheat the oven to Gas Mark 4/180°C/350°F. Cook in a Bain Marie until set.
6. Take out and allow to cool for 10 minutes. Pipe a line of whipped cream up the middle of the pudding, sprinkle the grated chocolate over the cream and dust the whole thing with icing sugar, serve.

**Sir Elton John &
David Furnish**

Pineapple Soufflé

This is a very easy way to do a soufflé and these **individual** ones are always a great success.

Makes 6 ramekins (12 cm diameter)

1 big Fairtrade pineapple
400 g caster sugar
20 g unsalted butter
40 g icing sugar
8 egg whites

1. First choose a ripe pineapple, peel it and cut it in four pieces lengthways, and discard the hard wooden core. Only use the juicy flesh and cut it into big chunks.
2. Cook 300 g of the caster sugar, with 20 g of water, in a sauté pan until golden and you have a caramel.
3. Take the pan off the heat and add your pineapple chunks (400 g is enough), and leave it to rest for 5 minutes (some of the caramel will solidify).

4. Put it back on the heat until all the caramel melts again with the juices that your pineapple creates while cooking. Pour it into a bowl and allow to cool.
5. When cooled reduce the pineapple mixture to a purée with a hand blender.
6. Melt your butter and then using a pastry brush, butter the inside of your ramekin and add some icing sugar so it sticks to the butter. Retrieve the excess by tapping the ramekin upside down on the table. (This process is called 'chemiser' and it's very important to do it, as it will help your soufflé to rise very high.)
7. Preheat your oven to Gas Mark 6/180°C and then follow the same procedure with all six ramekins.
8. Whisk your egg whites until very firm (before you whisk your egg whites, you need to have your ramekins ready). Add the rest of the caster sugar (100 g) and add a spoonful of this to your pineapple purée. Mix it well and then add your pineapple purée to the egg whites, folding gently with a wooden spoon.
9. Fill all six ramekins with the soufflé mix to 3 cm above the rim. If you want you can give it a rounder shape for a tidier look with a palette knife. Place them in the oven for 14 minutes (do not open the door while cooking) and serve at once. The soufflé will fall as it is taken out of the oven.

NOTE: If when you have filled your ramekins and you are left with some mix, it is because your egg whites were well whisked!

Our fruit tastes great, but in the Fairtrade system it's not enough just to produce quality. This fruit is also about the way it's produced. It's about the environment. It's about a fair system.

Bernardo Jaén, Pineapple Farmer, Costa Rica

Romas Foord

Skye Gyngell
Walnut & Honey Tart

The reason that I chose my Walnut and Honey Tart is that it is one of my favourite recipes. From the South of France, it is simple and an absolute **classic!** A Fair Feast is a very worthwhile cause and at Petersham Nurseries we feel strongly about acknowledging and making that **connection** between farming, growing and what appears on your table. Everybody should be recognised along the way, chefs have a commitment to farmers and we have to sustain that link.

1 cup caster sugar

¹/₂ cup water

400 g walnut halves (preferably fresh)

5 tablespoons of Fairtrade honey

4 tablespoons double cream

FOR THE PASTRY

250 g plain flour

zest of 1 Fairtrade lemon

30 g caster sugar

salt

125 g unsalted butter

1 whole egg

1 yolk

¹/₂ teaspoon vanilla extract

1 tablespoon iced water

1. First make the pastry. Mix together (either on a work surface or in a bowl) the flour, lemon zest, sugar and a pinch of salt.

2. Cut the butter into small cubes and put it into a well in the centre of the flour together with the whole egg, the yolk, vanilla extract and the water. Work everything together lightly until you have a homogenous whole. Do not overwork. Cover in clingfilm and refrigerate for 30 minutes. Alternatively if you have a Magimix, you can place all the ingredients in together and whiz.

3. Preheat the oven to Gas Mark 6/200°C. Sprinkle your work surface with flour; roll the pastry into an approximately 25 cm round. Line your tart tin with the pastry, pressing firmly into the sides with your thumb. Prick the base well with a fork and return to the fridge for a further 30 minutes. Blind bake in the oven for 15 minutes.

4. Meanwhile place the sugar and water in a small saucepan. Place over a medium heat and allow to caramelize to a beautiful golden brown. Add the walnuts, stirring well until all the nuts are well coated.

5. Away from the heat, add the honey and cream mixing them in well with a wooden spoon until lukewarm. Pour the mixture into the cooked tart shell – piling really high, so it looks really full and generous. We serve this tart simply with whipped cream.

AFRICA HAS LOST THE
EQUIVALENT OF 50 PENCE
FOR EVERY POUND RECEIVED
IN AID BECAUSE OF THE
FALLING PRICES IT GETS
FOR ITS COMMODITIES.

Richard & Judy
Sort of Bread & Butter Pud
(no bread & butter required)

Jim Marks

We tried this pud in the **Green Room** at our Studios and we persuaded the chef, Siobhan Boyle, to give us the recipe. She originally made it to use up pastries left over from a breakfast **meeting**. You don't have to use pastries though, basic croissants work well too. If you don't like apricots you can use raisins and sultanas, but apricot jam is the best for glazing no matter what fruit you use.

Makes 8 generous portions

12 croissants (or a combination of any 12 pastries, Danish type ones, brioche or panettone)
6 eggs
1 pint double cream
1 vanilla pod
1 tablespoon caster sugar
200 g dried apricots
1 jar of smooth apricot jam
caster sugar and cinnamon, to sprinkle

1. Set oven to Gas Mark 3/160°C and grease a 30 cm by 20 cm ovenproof dish.
2. To make the vanilla custard: beat the eggs and sugar together in a bowl and add the cream and seeds from the vanilla pod (seeds can be scraped out if you split pod in two lengthways).
3. To make the pudding: slice the pastries (a croissant can be sliced into five equal size pieces) and place a layer of pastry slices on the bottom of dish. Sprinkle with whole apricots and dust with cinnamon and caster sugar.
4. Keep layering until you run out of pastry slices. Ensure you finish with a layer of pastry slices (otherwise the fruit will burn). Dust the top with cinnamon and sugar.
5. Pour the custard over the top of the dish and leave to soak in for half an hour.
6. Place the pudding dish into a large roasting tin. Pour cold water into this tin, around the pudding dish (take care, the water is to go around the dish; don't over fill, the water must not go into the pudding! This is actually known as Bain Marie style of cooking).
7. Carefully place the roasting tin in the oven but if your oven is a safe height and sturdy you could do the water stuff at the oven! Cook for one hour, or until the custard is set.
8. Whilst the pudding is cooking, empty the whole jar of apricot jam into a saucepan and melt over a gentle heat. When your pudding is nearly ready, paint the jam on top to become a glaze; try and do this in the last five minutes of cooking time.
9. You can serve the dish with more double cream, crème fraîche, custard or a selection of fresh berries and some ice-cream – whatever you prefer.

The river is dirty and infested with crocodiles. Every year we lose women and children to serious injury or even death as they are collecting water. With the [Fairtrade] premium, we are hiring a contractor to drill bore holes so people can have safe and clean water near to their villages.

Brian Namata, Sugar Cane Grower, Malawi

Sam & Sam Clark
Orange & Almond Torta

Oranges, almonds and cinnamon are all **Moorish ingredients** that remind us so much of southern Spain and which are the main ingredients of this equally Moorish cake.

Serves 6

6 eggs, separated
240 g caster sugar
230 g almonds, almost finely ground
finely grated zest of 2 ¹/₂ Fairtrade oranges

FOR THE SYRUP
juice of 8 Fairtrade oranges
juice of 1 ¹/₂ Fairtrade lemons
1 whole cinnamon stick
caster sugar to taste

1. Preheat the oven to Gas Mark 4/180°C/ 350°F. Line a 23 cm spring form tin on the bottom and sides with greaseproof paper.

2. Keeping 1 tablespoon of caster sugar aside for later, mix the egg yolks and sugar together until pale. Then add the almonds and zest. Beat the egg whites and remaining tablespoon of sugar until stiff and carefully fold the sugar-egg mixture, trying not to knock the air out of the whites. The egg yolk/sugar mixture will seem very stiff at first, but keep folding in the egg whites and it will soon loosen up. Gently ease into the lined tin, place on the middle shelf of the oven and bake for about 60–70 minutes until the torta is golden on top and firm to the touch.

3. While the torta is in the oven, make the syrup. Place the orange juice, lemon juice and cinnamon stick in a saucepan with a handful of sugar, bring to a gentle boil and simmer for about 5 minutes. Taste. The syrup should be quite tart. Allow to cool and place in the fridge.

4. When the torta is ready, remove from the oven and cool completely on a rack before opening the spring form tin. Transfer to a plate and with a skewer, pierce four small holes in the top of the cake and pour half the syrup over the top. Serve with the rest of the syrup on the side.

ONE
BILLION
PEOPLE
LIVE IN
POVERTY.

Robin Matthews

Monica Ali
Halwa

*Halwa was originally a **royal sweet** dating from 18th-century Mughal India. Today it is a traditional sweet dish eaten throughout India and Bangladesh. It is usually served hot, although it can be served cold in summer. It is served with chapatis, parathas or loochis, usually for breakfast – though I only eat it as a pudding or as a snack. Don't worry if you remember horrible semolina puddings from **school days** and think that you loathe the stuff. This is a different proposition altogether.*

Serves 4

¹/₃ **litre water**
150 g **Fairtrade sugar**
5 **cardamoms, opened**
100 g **coarse semolina**
50 g **butter**
25 g **golden sultanas, washed and soaked**
25 g **roasted sliced almonds**
   or 15 g of roasted almonds and 15 g of green pistachio (available in Asian supermarkets)

1. Bring the water to boil in a pan along with the sugar and cardamoms and then simmer for 5 minutes on a low heat.
2. Dry fry the semolina in a heavy pan, stirring continuously until the semolina is a golden brown. Add the butter to the semolina and keep stirring on a low heat for about 5 minutes.
3. Add the sugared water, sultanas and nuts to the semolina and cook until the semolina thickens.
4. Turn down the heat and simmer for another 5 minutes. The semolina by this stage should have a thick grainy texture. If the halwa is too thick, add a little more water. If it is too runny, continue heating a little longer.

Robin Matthews

Antony Worrall Thompson
Tiramisú

I believe the FAIRTRADE Mark is changing the world, albeit too slowly. Everyone can help accelerate change by demanding our shops stock more Fairtrade goods. We have finally made them understand we want food that respects our environment. Now we must show them we want food that respects people. My Tiramisú recipe is both *indulgent and fair*. The recipe is centred on coffee – a market now offering consumers a wide variety of different estates, origins and blends from certified Fairtrade producer co-operatives. For this recipe, I would recommend using Union Coffee Roasters' marvellous Rwanda Maraba Bourbon – for the very real benefits it has brought its coffee farmers, and also its exceptional quality. Perfectly suited to brewing in the classic, stove top espresso style, this coffee combines sweet milk chocolate notes with *hints of fresh citrus* – alive and bright, it will really add an extra special something to this delicious treat.

Serves 4

3 egg yolks (preferably free-range or organic)
75 g (3 oz) caster sugar
2 x 250 g (9 oz) tubs of mascarpone cheese
85 ml (3 fl oz) Kahlua or coffee liqueur
200 ml (7 fl oz) cold strong Union Coffee Roasters' Rwanda Maraba Bourbon Fairtrade coffee, brewed in an espresso stovetop
14 boudoir or sponge finger biscuits
85 g (3 oz) plain Fairtrade 70% cocoa solids chocolate, finely grated
Fairtrade cocoa powder, for dusting

1. Place the egg yolks in a bowl with the caster sugar and beat together until pale and thickened, using an electric whisk. Add the mascarpone and whisk slowly until the mixture is pale and smooth. Pour in one tablespoon of the Kahlua or coffee liqueur and whisk gently to combine.

2. Mix the Rwanda Maraba Bourbon with the remaining Kahlua or liqueur in a shallow dish. Dip half of the boudoir or sponge finger biscuits into the coffee mixture and arrange in the bottom of four glass coffee cups, breaking them up as necessary. Spoon over half the mascarpone mixture and sprinkle half the chocolate on top. Repeat the layers and then cover each one with clingfilm. Chill for least for 2 hours or up to 24 hours is fine. Dust with cocoa powder just before serving.

Miki Duisterhof

Delia Smith
Banana & Walnut Loaf

This is a lovely, moist cake that keeps well and is perfect for picnics or packed lunches. In the summer it's **brilliant** served cut in thick slices and spread with clotted cream.

Serves 8

4 medium Fairtrade bananas (approximately 12 oz/350 g)
6 oz (175 g) walnut pieces
pinch of salt
1 rounded teaspoon baking powder
1 teaspoon ground cinnamon
4 oz (110 g) plain flour
4 oz (110 g) wholewheat flour
grated zest 1 Fairtrade orange
grated zest 1 Fairtrade lemon
4 oz (100 g) butter at room temperature
6 oz (175 g) soft dark brown sugar
2 large eggs at room temperature

FOR THE TOPPING
1 tablespoon Fairtrade demerara sugar
you will also need a 2 lb (900 g) loaf tin, lightly buttered

Preheat the oven to Gas Mark 4, 350°F/180°C.

"BEFORE YOU'VE FINISHED YOUR BREAKFAST THIS MORNING, YOU'LL HAVE RELIED ON HALF THE WORLD" – MARTIN LUTHER KING

Begin, as soon as the oven has preheated, by spreading the nuts out on a baking sheet and toasting them lightly in the oven for 7–8 minutes – use a timer so that you don't forget them. After that, remove them from the oven to a chopping board, let them cool briefly, then chop them fairly roughly. Now, in a bowl, peel and mash 3 of the bananas to a purée with a fork, and peel and chop the other one into ¹/₂ inch (1 cm) chunks.

Next you need to take a large mixing bowl and sift the salt, baking powder, cinnamon and both the flours into it, holding the sieve up high to give it a good airing, then adding the bran that's left in the sieve. Now simply add all the remaining ingredients (except the chopped banana and nuts) and, using an electric hand whisk, begin to beat the mixture, first on a slow speed for about half a minute, then increasing the speed to mix everything thoroughly and smoothly. Then lightly fold in the chopped banana and walnuts. You may need to add a drop of milk to give a mixture that drops easily off a spoon when you give it a sharp tap on the side of the bowl.

Next pile the mixture into the tin, level the top with the back of a spoon and sprinkle on the demerara sugar. Bake in the centre of the oven for 1 ¹/₄–1 ¹/₂ hours, until the cake feels springy in the centre. After that, remove it from the oven and let it cool for about 5 minutes before turning it out on a wire tray. Then let it get completely cold before serving or transferring it to a cake tin.

A Model of Trade

Fairtrade is not a charity but a voluntary model of trade. It aims to address the shocking injustices of conventional international trade, which heavily discriminates against already vulnerable producers and workers in the developing world. Fairtrade guarantees:

- fairer terms of trade and long-term contracts that ensure better prices for producers' goods (that cover the cost of production and provide a living income)

- financial security

- decent working conditions

- business support and local sustainability enabling them to regain control and work their way out of poverty.

Heston Blumenthal
Eton Mess

I am really honoured to be able to contribute to *A Fair Feast* supporting such an important cause. I hope you enjoy Eton Mess, **it's a fun recipe** that we serve at The Hinds Head Hotel, and which originally came from the tuck shop at Eton College.

To make 1 portion

1 whole Fairtrade banana
1 level teaspoon of lime juice and zest of 1 lime
50 ml double cream
half a vanilla pod
1 level teaspoon kirsch (not the red kirsch)
50 g meringue, broken up

1. Cut the banana in half. Using a folk, crush one half of the banana with the lime juice.
2. Whisk the cream into the banana purée, being very careful not to over whip it. Add the vanilla and kirsch, and fold them in.
3. Fold in your broken pieces of meringue and the other half of the banana that has been sliced thinly. Serve in a bowl, and scatter the lime zest over the whole dish.

Antonio Carluccio
Panna Cotta
– baked cream

A Fair Feast is a wonderful initiative and everybody with good sense should help to establish this venture. I am very glad to use the **delicious** Fairtrade ingredients whenever possible.

Serves 4–6

1 leaf of gelatine
500 ml (18 fl oz) single cream
45 g (1 ½ oz) Fairtrade sugar
1 vanilla pod
1 teaspoon vanilla essence
1 teaspoon dark rum
strips of candied orange peel or fresh berries to
   decorate

1. Soak the gelatine leaf in a little cold water until soft.
2. In a heavy based pan, mix the cream with the sugar and vanilla pod and essence. Bring to the boil.
3. Take off the heat and add the soaked gelatine leaf and the rum. Stir well until the gelatine has dissolved.
4. Pass through a fine sieve and pour into 4–6 dariole moulds. Put in the refrigerator to set.
5. To serve, decorate with small pieces of candied orange peel or, if you prefer, with fresh berries.

Matthew Leighton Photography

Prue Leith
Lemon Posset with Compote of Pears

Congratulations on a great idea, Vicky! Here is the simplest recipe in existence and one of the **nicest**.

Serves 3

FOR THE LEMON POSSET
¹/₂ pint double cream
1 tablespoon caster sugar
juice and finely grated zest of 1 Fairtrade lemon
 and 2 limes

1. Bring the cream and sugar to the boil. Boil, stirring for 4 minutes (watch it doesn't boil over).
2. Add zest and juice, stir and pour into little pots or glasses. Cool, then chill overnight, or for at least four hours. It will set like clotted cream.

COMPOTE OF PEARS FOR ON TOP
2 tablespoons redcurrant jelly
2 tablespoons Fairtrade sugar
2 Fairtrade pears, peeled and sliced in thick, even lengthways slices
1 teacup water

1. Dissolve the jelly and sugar in the water in a saucepan.
2. Add the pear slices and simmer until cooked and glassy, with the liquid reduced to a thick syrup. Pour on top of the Lemon Possets.

THE FAIRTRADE
FOUNDATION NOW
CERTIFIES OVER 900
PRODUCTS FROM
OVER 150 COMPANIES.

Spiced Winter Fruit with Nutmeg Ice Cream

I thoroughly agree with the fair trade initiative and look forward to seeing more products being added to the list. I have supported Oxfam for over 20 years and feel any tiny thing, done in the correct way, to redress the balance between western excess (of which I am a happy beneficiary) and Third World poverty makes the world a better place. My recipes are extremely simple, **I hope they are enjoyed**.

Serves 6

FOR THE SPICED WINTER FRUIT
100 g dried apricots
100 g prunes
100 g dried figs
50 g dried cranberries
2 Fairtrade Earl Grey teabags
¹/₂ teaspoon ground mixed spice
100 ml cranberry juice or Fairtrade orange juice
2 tablespoons Fairtrade demerara sugar
50 g finely chopped crystallized ginger

1. Put the fruit, mixed spice and tea bags in a large bowl, cover with boiling water. Leave to infuse for 10 minutes.
2. Remove the teabags and leave the mixture to stand overnight or for a minimum of 6 hours
3. Strain the liquid from the fruit into a saucepan; add the cranberry or orange juice, sugar and ginger. Put on the heat and boil for about 10 minutes or until the liquid becomes syrupy, add the fruit to the mixture and heat through, this will take about 5 minutes.
4. You can serve this either hot or cold with nutmeg ice cream or cream.

Sophie Conran

FOR THE NUTMEG ICE CREAM
(An ice-cream maker is essential for this recipe.
I used the Gelato Chef 2000 from Magimix)

5 egg yolks
100 g caster sugar
250 ml milk
1/2 teaspoon nutmeg
250 ml Jersey cream

1. Using your electric whisk, beat the egg yolks and sugar together until they are almost white.
2. Gently heat the milk and nutmeg, but don't boil, remove from the heat. Slowly pour about a third of the milk into the egg and sugar mixture, stirring with a wooden spoon. Pour back into the pan. Place on a gentle heat and stir continuously until it coats the back of the spoon. Remove from the heat, strain into a bowl and leave to cool.
3. Add the cream and whisk until it is completely mixed. Churn in an ice cream machine until thick, about 30 minutes, then freeze.

Before we farmers were cheated. People adjusted the scales. We got little money from the purchasing clerks and no bonuses. The farmers' welfare was neglected. I joined Kuapa [cocoa co-operative] because I saw it was the only organisation which could solve some of our problems – they trade without cheating, with the welfare of farmers at heart... Fairtrade deserves its name because it is fair. We would like more cocoa to be sold to Fairtrade because it means a better price for the producer.

Comfort Kumeah, Cocoa Farmer, Ghana

Sophie Baker

Roopa Gulati
Spiced Rice Pudding

Rice, one of the world's valued and versatile staples, is for many, a life-saving food. I've grown up on rice pudding – it's as popular at **Asian wedding** banquets as it is for Sunday family lunches. This recipe brings together sunshine ingredients and has hints of sweetly spiced Middle Eastern flavour.

Serves 4–6

100 g Fairtrade sugar
250 ml water
1 x 4 cm cinnamon stick
grated zest of 1 small Fairtrade orange
1 litre (250 ml) full cream milk
200 g risotto rice, such as Arborio
1 tablespoon thick double cream
dash of rosewater

FOR THE FRUIT SALAD
2 Fairtrade mangoes, diced
1 Fairtrade orange, segmented
2 tablespoons Fairtrade organic ginger wine
1 tablespoon stem ginger, finely chopped
1 tablespoon syrup from the stem ginger

1. Dissolve the sugar in the water along with the cinnamon stick and zest. Bring to a simmer and cook down until the syrup has reduced by half – around 3–5 minutes.
2. Pour in the milk and bring to a boil. Turn down the heat a tad, sprinkle in the rice and simmer until the rice is really soft, stirring occasionally. This should take about 20 minutes. If it looks like it's getting a tad dry, add a dash more milk.
3. Remove the pan from the heat and stir in the cream. Remove the cinnamon stick and add rosewater to taste. Turn the pudding into a bowl and leave on one side to cool.
4. Serve chilled, with the fruit salad. To prepare the salad, tip the prepared fruit into a bowl and add the ginger wine, stem ginger and syrup. Stir well and chill for an hour or so before serving.

Gus Philgate

Rose Elliot
Mango, Cardamom & Pistachio Fool

This is **gorgeous**, but for a less-rich version, use thick Greek yogurt, or half yogurt and half cream, whipped together.

Serves 4

1/2 teaspoon cardamom seeds
1 large, ripe Fairtrade mango
300 ml (1/2 pint) double cream
2 tablespoons shelled pistachios, roughly chopped

1. Crush the cardamoms using a pestle and mortar, or with the end of a rolling pin on a board, removing the outer husks. Set aside.
2. Make two cuts in the mango straight down about 5 mm either side of the stalk, to cut the flesh from the flat stone. Then peel off the skin and cut the flesh into rough pieces; remove as much flesh from around the stone as you can.
3. Put all the mango flesh into a food processor, along with the cardamom, and whiz to a purée.
4. Whip the cream until it will stand in stiff peaks, then gently fold in the mango puree, not too thoroughly, to give a pretty marbled effect. Spoon the mixture into four glasses and top with the pistachios.

SALES OF FAIRTRADE GOODS IN THE UK HAVE GROWN BY OVER 50 PER CENT DURING THE PAST YEAR.

George Alagiah
Pancakes with Coconut Filling

*My mother used to serve these pancakes as a treat for breakfast or for what she used to call "tiffin" – a snack in the afternoon. The first time I had it was as a **child in Sri Lanka**; whenever we have it now it reminds me of her home-cooking. I've had to amend the recipe because some of the ingredients are not easily available here. Also, I've had to experiment with quantities. All I got when I checked with my aunts was a vague, "just put enough so it tastes nice"!*

Serves 4–6

FOR THE PANCAKES
(Everybody has their own way of making them;
   I use this recipe).
100 g plain flour
a tiny pinch of salt
2 large eggs
200 ml milk
75 ml water
butter to grease the pan

FOR THE FILLING
100 g desiccated coconut
½ cup hot water (not boiling)
4 tablespoons date syrup (my mother used
   jaggery or kitul pani from the kitul palm tree)
60 g roasted cashew nuts or Fairtrade brazil nuts
   (my mother used roasted mung beans)

1. To make the pancake batter, mix the flour and salt. Break the eggs into it and start whisking. Pour the milk and water (mixed) little by little. Keep mixing until you have a nice smooth consistency. Leave to one side.

2. Put the coconut into a small bowl. Add the water little by little. It should all get absorbed. Add the date syrup to the coconut (you can vary the amount according to taste). Crush the cashew or brazil nuts in a mortar and add to the coconut. Mix all the ingredients. Leave to one side.

3. Now cook the pancakes. I use a non-stick frying pan. Pour 2 tablespoons of the pancake mix into the pan and tilt it around till it has spread across the bottom of the pan. Wait till it has begun to turn golden and then – here's the tricky bit – flip it over. (We have family competitions to see who can do it without ending up with a half-cooked pancake draped over the side of the cooker.) Once both sides are cooked, keep warm in the oven. Repeat the process until you have about four to six pancakes.

4. Put the filling in the middle of the pancakes and roll them over.

5. Enjoy!

PROPER ECONOMIC PRICES
SHOULD BE FIXED NOT AT THE
LOWEST POSSIBLE LEVEL, BUT
AT A LEVEL SUFFICIENT TO
PROVIDE PRODUCERS WITH
PROPER NUTRITIONAL AND
OTHER STANDARDS
- JOHN MAYNARD KEYNES, 1944

Spiced Pineapple & Lacy Ginger Biscuit Sandwiches with Mascarpone Cream

I devised this pudding one freezing Sunday afternoon in January with my spice-a-holic 11-year-old nephew, Angus. We were certainly a lot warmer when we finished than we were when we started! The pineapple compote is spectacular and goes brilliantly with ginger or vanilla ice cream if you have any of it left over. Don't be put off by the long list of ingredients – this is wonderfully simple to make and it looks very impressive. Ask any 11-year-old. You can make all of the components up to 6 hours ahead and assemble them at the last minute.

Serves 6–8

FOR THE BISCUITS

80 g soft brown sugar

80 g unsalted butter

2 tablespoons golden syrup

1 tablespoon Fairtrade orange juice

50 g plain flour

2 tbsp small pieces of crystallized ginger

1 teaspoon ground ginger

1 teaspoon finely grated Fairtrade orange zest

pinch of salt

FOR THE SPICED PINEAPPLE

500 ml unsweetened pineapple juice

40 g Fairtrade demerara sugar

6 cardamom pods, split

1 teaspoon pink peppercorns

2 cloves

1 star anise

$1/2$ red chilli (split lengthways, with seeds)

1 cinnamon stick

1 Fairtrade pineapple, peeled, cored and cut into chunks

FOR THE MASCARPONE CREAM

250 g mascarpone

1 tablespoon caster sugar

1 tablespoon tequila

100 ml whipping cream

2 tablespoons toasted, unsweetened dessicated coconut

Debora Robertson

1. To make the biscuits, first line two large baking sheets with parchment. In a medium saucepan over a medium heat, stir the sugar, butter, golden syrup and orange juice until everything is melted and well combined. Boil for 1 minute. Remove the pan from the heat and stir in the flour, crystallized ginger, ground ginger, orange zest and a pinch of salt. Beat until the batter is smooth. Allow to cool and thicken. Preheat the oven to Gas Mark 4/180°C/350°F.

2. Scoop out teaspoons of the dough and roll into balls the size of small marbles. Place on the prepared sheets approximately 10 cm apart to allow room for them to spread. Bake for 9–10 minutes until the biscuits are lacy and golden brown. Quickly transfer the parchment to a wire rack and allow the biscuits to cool.

3. To prepare the pineapple, put the first eight ingredients in a medium-sized pan and bring to a simmer over a medium heat. Simmer for about 5 minutes until it has reduced by about a third. Add the pineapple chunks and simmer for 20 minutes until the pineapple is slightly translucent. With a slotted spoon, remove the pineapple pieces and transfer them to a plate to cool. Strain the liquid and return it to the pan. Boil until reduced to about 150 ml – this takes about 5 minutes.

4. Beat the mascarpone with the sugar and tequila until smooth. In a separate bowl, whip the cream until it forms soft peaks. Gently fold the whipped cream into the mascarpone mixture.

5. On each plate, place one of the biscuits topped with a big blob of the mascarpone cream. Place a few pineapple chunks in the cream and top with another biscuit. Repeat the process once more so you have a double-decker sandwich of biscuits, cream and pineapple. Drizzle a little of the pineapple syrup over the top and sprinkle on some toasted coconut.

Lucy Young
Lime Coconut Creams

Dave Woolford

These are very quick, but they are fairly rich, so I have made them quite small. They're perfect for a large dinner party as they are served cold. Be careful not to overcook as bubbles will appear and they will taste curdled: they should be smooth and melt in your mouth.

Serves 6

butter for greasing
2 x 200 ml (7 fl oz) or 1 x 400 ml (12 fl oz) coconut cream from a carton
150 ml (5 fl oz) double cream
finely grated zest of 1 lime and lime segments
3 egg yolks
1 egg
100 g (4 oz) caster sugar

1. Preheat the oven to Gas Mark 3/160°C/325°F. Butter six timbale moulds or size 1 ramekins, and sit them in a small roasting tin.
2. Measure the coconut cream, double cream and lime zest into a saucepan, and bring to simmering point, but do not allow to boil.
3. Whisk the egg yolks, egg and caster sugar together in a bowl until combined. Pour in the hot cream mixture and whisk until well blended.
4. Divide the mixture evenly between the timbale moulds. Pour boiling water into the roasting tin until it comes halfway up the sides of the moulds (this is a bain-marie). Bake in the preheated oven for about 20–25 minutes until just set but still with a slight wobble. Set aside to cool and transfer to the fridge to set.
5. Dip the moulds in hot water (to help the creams come out) and turn on to plates. Garnish with fresh mint and lime segments.

TO COOK IN THE AGA

Slide the bain-marie on to the lowest set of runners in the roasting oven for about 5–8 minutes (do not let the creams bubble or go brown). Transfer to the simmering oven for about 25–30 minutes until just set. Set aside to cool.

NOTE: Coconut cream is UHT and comes in a carton, available in all good supermarkets in the Indian/Thai section. Do not use coconut milk, as the creams will not set firm enough to turn out.

IN 2002, THE AVERAGE PRICE
OF ORDINARY BANANAS IN UK
SUPERMARKETS WAS £1.12 PER
KILO. BY THE START OF 2005,
THE PRICE WAS JUST 74p PER
KILO, A DROP OF 33%. WHO PAYS
THE PRICE OF OUR BARGAINS?

Adam Lawrence

John Burton Race
Coffee Caramels

I believe that in this day and age every single person around the world should have access to nutritional and sustainable food sources. It is therefore an honour for me to be associated with such a worthy cause as A Fair Feast. *Crème caramel is one of the most famous classic desserts. Adding coffee to it gives another dimension. Try it – you'll be hooked.*

Serves 6

FOR THE CARAMEL
120 g caster sugar
90 ml water

FOR THE CUSTARD
60 g caster sugar
4 eggs (small)
10 g Fairtrade instant coffee granules
500 ml milk

1. First make the caramel. Put the sugar and half the water in a small saucepan and place it on the stove to boil. When the sugar starts to colour (it will become dark golden), quickly remove the pan from the heat and add the remaining water. This will stop the sugar from becoming darker. Put the pan back on the heat. Remove it as soon as it starts to boil again. Pour a little of the caramel into the bottom of six lightly buttered 8 cm ramekin dishes and allow to set.

2. Preheat the oven to Gas Mark 1/2/120°C/250°F. Pour the milk into a saucepan and warm. Put the sugar and eggs in a bowl and whisk them until smooth. Stir the coffee granules into the warm milk and then pour the coffee-flavoured milk into the eggs, stirring all the time. With a ladle, remove all the surfacing foam and discard.

3. Pour the mixture into the ramekins, cover them with clingfilm, and put in a deep roasting tray. Carefully pour boiling water into the tray to within 1 cm of the top of the ramekins, then place in the oven for about 35 minutes until the custard has set. Remove the ramekins from the baking tray, allow them to cool, then refrigerate for at least 4 hours before serving.

4. To serve, remove the clingfilm from the ramekins. Gently press down around the edges of the custards and shake them free. Turn them upside down into the centre of a small bowl, allowing all of the caramel to pour out over the top of the desserts.

Gus Philgate

Silvana Franco
Mint & Choc Chip Ice Cream

A simple version of the classic flavour, only this time it's not bright green and it does contain real mint.

Serves 4–6

50 g caster sugar
large handful of fresh mint leaves
100 ml water
250 g carton of mascarpone
500 ml fresh ready-made custard
150 ml double cream, lightly whipped
100 g good quality Fairtrade dark chocolate,
   roughly chopped

1. Place the sugar in a small pan with 100 ml of water and heat together, stirring, until the sugar dissolves. Leave to cool.
2. Finely chop the mint and stir into the cooled syrup.
3. Put the mascarpone into a bowl and gradually beat in the cooled mint syrup (don't add it all at once or you'll never get the lumps out). Now stir in the custard.
4. Next gently fold the cream into the mixture, along with the chopped chocolate.
5. Churn in an ice-cream machine until firm or pour the mixture into a freezer container and cover with a tight-fitting lid.
6. Place the container in the freezer for 2 hours, then beat with a fork to break up the ice crystals.
7. Return to the freezer and repeat the process after another 2 hours.
8. Return to the freezer until completely frozen.

WE EAT AN ESTIMATED 60 BILLION DOLLARS WORTH OF CHOCOLATE EVERY YEAR

Mitzie Wilson
Banana & Date Loaf

*I have been making this cake for years. Whenever I have slightly blackened over-ripe bananas, I use them as an excuse to make this **moist yummy** cake. The flavour of bananas really comes through. If you prefer, omit the dates, or add chocolate chips instead.*

Makes a 1 kg (2 lb) loaf that cuts into 10 slices

125 g (4 oz) dried pitted dates
500 g (1 lb) ripe Fairtrade bananas,
 about 3 altogether
125 g (4 oz) plain flour
125 g (4 oz) wholemeal flour
2 teaspoons baking powder
125 g (4 oz) butter, softened
90 g (3 oz) light or dark Muscovado sugar
2 eggs, size 3, beaten
1 tablespoon milk, optional
60 g (2 oz) sweetened dried banana chips

1. Preheat the oven to Gas Mark 4/180°C. Grease a 1 kg (2 lb) loaf tin and line the base with greaseproof paper.
2. Finely chop the dates and set aside. Peel and mash the bananas into a large bowl, then add the flours, baking powder, softened butter, sugar and eggs and beat with a wooden spoon for 1 to 2 minutes until just blended and smooth.
3. Add the milk, if necessary, to give a soft dropping consistency, stir in the dates. Spread the mixture in the prepared tin, level the top and sprinkle with banana chips.
4. Bake in the centre of the oven for 1 hour or until firm to the touch, and a skewer inserted in the centre comes out clean.
5. Allow the loaf to cool in the tin for 10 minutes, then turn it out on to a wire rack, peel off the lining paper and leave to cool completely.

STORING AND FREEZING: Store for up to one week in a cake tin. Freeze whole or sliced in a plastic bag or airtight container for up to 3 months. Defrost the whole loaf for 5 to 6 hours at room temperature and the slices for 1 hour at room temperature.

BANANAS ARE THE
BIGGEST-SELLING FRUIT
IN THE UK, AND THE
MOST VALUABLE
GROCERY PRODUCT
FOR SUPERMARKETS.

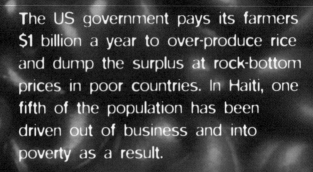

The US government pays its farmers $1 billion a year to over-produce rice and dump the surplus at rock-bottom prices in poor countries. In Haiti, one fifth of the population has been driven out of business and into poverty as a result.

Chris Martin - singer

chocoholics' corner

Jemma Kidd
Luxury Real Hot Chocolate

Greater awareness in Fairtrade products can only be a good thing. Farmers in developing countries absolutely deserve to be helped and their products promoted. As a consumer I want to know what I am buying, where it has come from and moreover that the product is 'Fairtrade'. On a **cold winter's evening** when I want to have something delicious and indulgent I make real hot chocolate; the recipe is very easy and the trick is always to use the best quality ingredients you can afford.

This makes enough for 4 cups

550 ml whole organic milk
50 ml bottled water
60 g caster sugar
1 x 100 g Fairtrade plain dark bittersweet chocolate (finely sliced with a serrated knife) or as an alternative try using Green & Blacks Maya Gold Fairtrade chocolate for a more exotic taste
28 g Fairtrade cocoa powder
dash (to taste) of 7-year-old Havana rum

1. In a saucepan stir together the milk, water and sugar then bring to the boil over a medium heat. Add the chopped chocolate and cocoa powder and bring to the boil again whisking until the chocolate and cocoa powder are dissolved and the mixture has thickened.
2. Reduce to a very low heat and blend for 5 minutes with a wand mixer or whirl the hot chocolate in a standard blender for half a minute, until thick and foamy. Then add a dash of 7-year-old Havana rum, or more according to taste.

Ruth Rogers & Rose Gray
15-Minute Chocolate Cake

Johnnie Shand Kydd

This is probably the easiest and **quickest** chocolate cake we've ever done. It is great for a dinner party when you're short of time but still want to make the pudding yourself.

Serves 8

450 g Fairtrade chocolate 70% cocoa solids
215 g unsalted butter
6 eggs, organic

1. Preheat the oven to Gas Mark 7/220°C. Using extra butter, grease a 25 cm spring form cake tin, and line with parchment paper.
2. Break the chocolate into pieces, and melt with the butter in a bowl over simmering water.
3. In a separate bowl, over simmering water, beat the eggs until they start to thicken, then remove from the heat and continue beating until firm peaks form.
4. Fold half the eggs into the melted chocolate, then fold in the remainder. Pour the mixture into the tin and cover with buttered foil.
5. Place in a bain-marie of very hot water. It is essential, if the cake is to cook evenly, that the water comes halfway up the sides of the tin.
6. Bake for 5 minutes, remove the foil, and bake for a further 10 minutes until just set. Remove from the water and cool in the tin. Turn out when completely cool.

NOTE: The butter, chocolate and eggs should all be at room temperature. If using an electric mixer, warm the bowl and beat close to the stove, while the chocolate is melting.

Nigella Lawson

James Merrell

Makes about 8 slices

2 small or 1 large thin-skinned Fairtrade orange,
    approx. 375 g total weight
6 eggs
1 heaped teaspoon baking powder
½ teaspoon bicarbonate of soda
200 g ground almonds
250 g caster sugar
50 g Fairtrade cocoa
Fairtrade orange peel for decoration if wished

*This has a very simple origin, which is just as it
should be for a very simple cake. I think more people
tell me they did my Clementine cake in* How To Eat
*than any other recipe, and when I was having some
friends round for dinner one night, I thought I'd get
ahead the evening before and try out a chocolate
version. There's something about its citrussy wetness
and yet the lightness you get from not using flour that
makes this **perfect to toy with over a cup of coffee**
at the end of an evening. And it's useful to bring out
when you have to entertain the gluten-intolerant. In
fact, though, its sombre plainness makes it really the
antithesis of any dinner-party gateau, if you want a
cake to hang around the kitchen (it lasts for an almost
spookily long time) to be sliced as mood and appetite
dictate, then this is it.*

Chocolate Orange Cake

1. Put the whole orange or oranges in a pan with some cold water, bring to the boil and cook for 2 hours or until soft. Drain and, when cool, cut the oranges in half and remove any big pips. Then pulp everything – pith, peel and all – in a food processor.

2. Once the fruit is cold, or near cold (though actually I most often cook the oranges the day before I make the cake), preheat the oven to Gas Mark 4/180°C. Butter and line a 20 cm spring form tin.

3. Add the eggs, baking powder, bicarbonate of soda, almonds, sugar and cocoa to the orange in the food processor. Run the motor until you have a cohesive cake mixture, but still slightly knobbly with the flecks of puréed orange.

4. Pour and scrape into the cake tin and bake for an hour, by which time a cake tester should come out pretty well clean. Check after 45 minutes because you may have to cover with foil to prevent the cake burning before it is cooked through, or indeed it may need a little less than an hour; it all depends on your oven.

5. Leave the cake to get cool in the tin, on a cooling rack. When the cake is cold you can take it out of the tin. Decorate with strips of orange peel or coarsely grated zest if you so wish, but it is darkly beautiful in its plain, unadorned state.

NOTE: You can leave out the baking powder and bicarb if dietary requirements make that desirable, but in that case, I'd use a 23 cm tin instead and expect it to need slightly less cooking time.

I have five children and because of Fairtrade I can afford to send them to school, provide them with medical care when they are sick and plan for my family's future.

Siswandi Idris, Coffee Farmer, Aceh, Indonesia

The **Benefits** of **Fairtrade**

Globally, over 400 producer organisations in 49 countries benefit from the international Fairtrade system. In 2004 alone, they received an estimated $50 million more from Fairtrade sales than they would have done if they had sold the same products on the conventional market.

Fairtrade benefits producers in a whole range of ways:

- Regular income: Long-term contracts allow a real sense of security rather than being at the mercy of unstable market prices. Instead of enduring periods of hunger, food is now secure for these families. Instead of living hand to mouth, they can plan for a future.

- Workers' pay and conditions: Being paid at least the national minimum wage and receiving health and social security benefits would have been inconceivable before Fairtrade.

- Cleaner environment: Producers need to meet Fairtrade's environmental standards. This is achieved by education concerning environmental issues, which is proving so effective that some farmers are even clearing up litter left by non-Fairtrade producers!

- Housing: Thanks to Fairtrade, instead of living in decrepit state-owned housing, we are hearing of producers planning for and building their own homes.

- Health and sanitation: Some communities had no sanitation facilities until Fairtrade farmers began to help by installing toilets, clean water supplies and improving local health centres.

- Increased efficiency: As a result of Fairtrade sales, farmers are in a position to begin to improve roads and irrigation, benefiting the whole community, including non-Fairtrade farmers.

- Better business: Fairtrade farmers have invested in new equipment, improved quality control and established training programmes, making them stronger in winning a better deal from the market.

FROM CHOCOLATE TO BANANAS, MANY PRODUCERS AROUND THE WORLD CANNOT AFFORD TO EAT THE VERY FRUITS OF THEIR LABOUR.

Jo Pratt
White Chocolate & Espresso Mousse

Jeremy Hudson

biscotti biscuits, to serve
2 hot shots of espresso (using Fairtrade coffee)
2 egg whites
300 ml double cream
4 tablespoons water
200 g Fairtrade white chocolate, broken into pieces

Serves 4

The satisfying feeling you have when you cook and eat great tasty food is hard to beat, but for me it's really topped off when I know the ingredients I'm using are going to contribute towards helping farmers, their families and community live a better life. No matter how small the ingredient – it all helps towards feeding those who are truly in need.

My deliciously rich white chocolate mousse looks so gorgeous served in coffee cups with saucers, then just before serving you pour over a shot of espresso coffee. The coffee melts into the mousse giving it a really lovely fluffy topping like a cappuccino.

1. Place the chocolate and water in a bowl over a pan of gently simmering water and leave to slowly melt. Remove from the heat, stir and leave to cool for about 5 minutes.

2. Whip the cream until it thickens to form soft peaks and, in a separate bowl, whisk the egg whites until it also forms soft peaks.

3. Pour the melted chocolate into the whipped cream and gently stir in. Fold in the egg whites before spooning into the coffee cups, making sure you leave at least 1 cm of a rim at the top for the coffee.

4. Ideally chill in the fridge for about 2–3 hours to set, but they can be eaten straight away if you are really desperate. Just before serving, sit the cups on the saucers, pour over hot espresso and enjoy straight away with the biscotti biscuits on the side to dip in.

A LITTLE TIP... Try a splash of your favourite liqueur in the espresso. I love the orangy flavour of Gran Marnier but whisky, brandy or Tia Maria are just as good.

Bob Morphew

Kim Morphew
Mochana Tart

I love cooking for my family and friends, and by using Fairtrade products we can really help to feed those who are truly in need. I'm a chocoholic – but when choosing chocolate I only ever use Fairtrade, not only for the pure quality of the cocoa but also because it guarantees a better deal for Third World producers. It's my small way of helping. So, of course I've created a chocolate dessert! My recipe for Mochana Tart has a luxurious, velvety chocolate, coffee and banana filling in a crunchy flapjack shell. Delicious! You only need a little and don't worry it is guilt free because by cooking this recipe you then help to make a difference. Fairtrade products are simply wonderful and I hope by enjoying the Mochana Tart it will open your eyes to the whole range of products available. So all that's left to do is tuck in and enjoy!!

Serves 8–10

2 x 150 g box Co-op Fairtrade mini flapjack bites
2 x 100 g Divine Fairtrade dark chocolate (at least 70% cocoa)
25 g (1 oz) unsalted butter
1 x 397 g can of condensed milk
1 x 300 g packet of soft cream cheese
2 teaspoons Fairtrade instant coffee dissolved in 1 tablespoon boiling water
3 Fairtrade bananas

1. Preheat the oven to Gas Mark 5/190°C/fan oven 170°C. Grease and base line a 20 cm (8 inch) loose bottom sandwich tin with baking parchment.
2. Whiz the mini flapjacks in a food processor until really fine. Spoon into the prepared tin and press into the base and sides with the back of a spoon to make a shell. Bake in the oven for 5 minutes. Allow to cool.
3. Heat 175 g chocolate in a bowl over a pan of barely simmering water until melted. Set aside. Melt the butter in a non-stick saucepan and add the condensed milk. Heat gently for 10 minutes, stirring continuously, until thick.
4. Put the cream cheese in a bowl and whisk to loosen. Add the thick condensed milk, dissolved coffee and melted chocolate and whisk until smooth.
5. Peel and slice 1 banana and arrange in the base of the flapjack shell. Spoon over the chocolate mixture and level the top. Chill for about 8 hours or overnight. When ready to serve, slice the remaining bananas and grate the remaining chocolate. Use to decorate the tart and serve immediately.

A GHANAIAN COCOA FARMER GETS ONLY 1.2 PER CENT OF THE PRICE WE PAY FOR A BAR OF CHOCOLATE. BETWEEN 1996 AND 2000 GHANA INCREASED COCOA PRODUCTION BY ALMOST A THIRD BUT WAS PAID A THIRD LESS.

Jamie Oliver
Fairtrade Chocolate Pots

Harry Borden

The beauty of this dessert is that it is so smooth, silky and rich. However, if you want to lighten the texture to make it into more of a mousse, then follow the recipe here but fold in 2 stiffly whipped egg whites before pouring into the pots. Small servings are the key – I generally use espresso cups as they're the ideal size. Chocolate pots are brilliant for dinner parties as you can make them up the day before and stick them in the fridge until needed. Chocolate pots are especially delicious when made with Fairtrade chocolate. Foods with the FAIRTRADE Mark are produced with pride, bursting with taste. The FAIRTRADE Mark is your independent guarantee that producers in developing countries receive a fair deal.

Serves 4

285 ml (½ pint) single cream
200 g (7 oz) Fairtrade dark chocolate (70% cocoa solids)
2 large egg yolks
3 tablespoons brandy, the best you can get
20 g (¾ oz) butter

1. In a thick-bottomed pan, heat the cream until nearly boiling. Remove and set aside for 1 minute before snapping in your chocolate. Stir in until melted and smooth.
2. Once melted, beat in your egg yolks and brandy and stir until smooth. Allow to cool slightly before stirring in the butter until the mixture is smooth.
3. Pour into individual serving pots.

P.S. Sometimes if you add the butter when the chocolate isn't cool enough it will make the chocolate look as if it has split. To rectify this, allow the mixture to cool a little longer before whisking in a little cold milk until you have a smooth consistency again.

Sue Lawrence
Fairtrade Brownies

*This brownie recipe is a great family favourite. But when enhanced with Fairtrade raisins, nuts and honeycomb, it is even more **fabulous**. My wish is that more and more people buy Fairtrade products. It is one of the easiest ways for us in the **comfort** of our own well-stocked kitchens, to help tackle world poverty. And it is no hardship for us, because the products also taste so good!*

Makes 16–20 brownies

350 g Fairtrade dark chocolate
200 g butter
250 g unrefined dark muscovado sugar
3 large free-range eggs
90 g plain flour, sifted
1 teaspoon baking powder
a pinch of salt
small handful dried apricots, chopped
small handful each of Fairtrade brazils
(chopped); chocolate raisins; chocolate
honeycomb

1. Melt the chocolate and butter together (I do this in the microwave but it can be done in a bowl over a pan of gently simmering water) then stir until smooth.

2. Place the sugar in a bowl; if it is slightly lumpy, either break it up with your fingers or warm very, very slightly in the microwave (for a couple of turns) then stir it.

3. Add the eggs to the sugar, one at a time, beating after each addition. Slowly add this to the melted chocolate mixture, stirring well.

4. Sift in the flour, baking powder and a pinch of salt and gently fold together.

5. Tip into a lined, deep 23 cm (9 inch) brownie pan, scatter over the various flavourings, poke them all down under the batter and bake at Gas Mark 3/ 170ºC/325ºF for 35–40 minutes, or until a wooden cocktail stick inserted into the middle comes out with some moist crumbs adhering. It should also feel just firm when you place the palm of your hand gently on top.

6. Remove the tin to a wire rack and allow to cool for half an hour or so then cut into 16 or 20 brownies. Leave until completely cold before removing the brownies.

Why do we need Fairtrade?

World trade harbours the potential to lift millions out of poverty. It should, and can, enhance and enrich all of our lives. At present, it is being manipulated as a force to exploit and oppress millions of people and ravage the environment. The price of the prosperity of the global North is the increasing mass poverty in the South, where the majority of the world's population live. The instability created by the widening chasm of inequality between these extremes of rich and poor threatens to engulf us all. But it doesn't have to be this way.

Fairtrade enables consumers to use their purchasing power by buying more directly from producers, and offering them a better deal. This makes the difference between survival and starvation for hundreds of thousands of people across the world – indefensible and unsustainable unfair terms of trade are no longer being tolerated. Sharp fluctuations in world prices, as well as an overall long-term decline in commodity prices have had a devastating impact on the lives of millions of producers. Many are forced into crippling debt and have to work even harder to produce more of their crop, resulting in oversupply and thus, extremely frustratingly, even lower prices. Fairtrade provides stable prices and secure long-term contracts whilst also helping producers diversify into other crops by offering capital, advice and support. Instead of being powerless in the face of world prices, they can reclaim control over their own futures.